Arts and Crafts Walks in
Broadway and Chipping Campden

Written by Alan Crawford and designed by Sue Haigh

The Guild of Handicraft Trust
Chipping Campden, Gloucestershire
2002

Cover
F. L. Griggs, 'Footbridge in the pastures', 1918,
from *Campden: XXIV engravings* (1940) (Courtesy of the British Library, LR 28a21)

Inside front cover
Repairing the Norman Chapel, Broad Campden, c. 1906
(Photograph by Jesse Taylor, courtesy of the Guild of Handicraft Trust)

Back cover detail
F. L. Griggs, 'The Landgate brook and cottage in Sheep Street', 1918,
from *Campden: XXIV engravings* (1940)

Acknowledgments

Many people have helped me with this book, and I would particularly like to thank
Trevor Chinn, Peter Cormack, Avril Denton, David and Diana Evans, Charlotte Gere, Mary Greensted,
David Hart, Sorrel Hershberg, Carol Jackson, Frank and Alice Johnson, Jerrold Northrop Moore,
Geoffrey Powell, Michael Pyment, Natasha Roderick-Jones, Alistair and Rosemary Voaden,
Allan Warmington, the Welch family, and John and Brenda Williams.

For permissions to quote from copyright material, I am grateful to Felicity Ashbee
(the papers of C. R. and Janet Ashbee) and to Jane Wilgress (the papers of Alec Miller).
I am grateful to Barbara Griggs for permission to reproduce her father's work as illustrations.

My special thanks go to Susan Crawford for her support for this book.

ALAN CRAWFORD, JUNE 2002

Contents

The Arts and Crafts movement in the Cotswolds

This is the story of an invasion in which the invaders came armed not with guns but with sketchbooks. They invaded a country which contained (almost) no enemies. And when the war was over, victory seemed the same thing as defeat, for they were captured by the countryside, which was what they had wanted all along. The territory over which they marched was roughly the eastern half of Gloucestershire, which takes its name from the bare upland country known as the wolds. Modern tourists and those who retire to the Cotswolds are drawn by the beauty of the landscape and of the towns and villages built of grey-brown Cotswold stone. But it was not always so. Here is William Cobbett, travelling through Gloucestershire in the early 19th century, and coming out of Cirencester: 'I came up hill into a country, apparently formerly a down or common, but now divided into large fields by stone walls. Anything so ugly I have never seen before.' [1]

This essay traces the part which artists and craftsmen played in this shift of taste in the years round 1900. It takes account of the Cotswolds as a whole but, for the sake of the walks which follow, it concentrates on Broadway and Chipping Campden in the north, and only makes passing mention of many important workshops in the south.

The invaders were the furniture makers, weavers, architects, potters, metalworkers, painters, printers, jewellers, stained-glass artists and bookbinders of the Arts and Crafts movement. They believed in handwork and in making simple, individual things, not products to be endlessly multiplied. And they looked to the past for inspiration in their work, adopting and adapting old, pre-industrial ways of making, and calling them 'crafts'. Their contemporaries probably thought of them as cranks, but their views shaped architecture and decorative art in England for several decades round 1900. Arts and Crafts was the progressive movement of the time. Between the wars it still inspired craft activity, though by then it was no longer progressive.

In 1800 roughly three quarters of the population of England lived in rural towns and villages, mainly in the agricultural south. Over the next hundred years industrialisation and population growth so swelled the size of towns and cities that by 1900 roughly three quarters lived in or around large cities, many of them in the industrial midlands and the north. This did not mean that the countryside was depopulated, but that the population increase was taken up in urban areas. England had become a mainly urban nation, and the country was increasingly seen from the city: as an economic problem when English agriculture could not compete in price against wheat from the United States and meat from South America and Australia; as 'the countryside', a place to visit; and, thanks to Romanticism, as the spiritual antithesis of the city. It began to be associated more with the past than with the present.

Sketching party in the Cotswolds **a watercolour by May Francis, c. 1900** *(Courtesy of Cheltenham Art Gallery and Museum and Bridgeman Art Library)*

The Arts and Crafts, like almost all modern movements in art, was urban. Its principal organisations and networks were in London; its members mostly lived and worked in cities. But its imagination was deeply rural. They filled their work with flowers and trees and birds and leaves. And the countryside was the theatre of their anti-modernism. If they dreamed of an innocent craftsmanlike past before the Industrial Revolution, where could it be but in the countryside? The conviction grew in some of them – and it was always only a small proportion – that they must leave the city and find the true life of craftsmanship in the country. Craft workshops were established in the Lake District, Surrey and Sussex, and most of all in the Cotswolds. This movement 'back to the land' was full of hope and creativity. But it was also full of naïveté: they thought that they were discovering these places. And of irony: it was the railway, the driving force of industrialisation, which took them there and made their work possible. And of misunderstandings: blinkered by Romanticism, they did not understand that the country too could be modern.

The first Arts and Crafts settler was the movement's best-known figure, the stocky poet, designer, shopkeeper and socialist, William Morris. In 1871 he and the painter D. G. Rossetti took a tenancy of Kelmscott Manor, near Lechlade on the edge of the Cotswolds, a homely-looking stone house built around 1600 and added to about sixty years later. It was to be a second home and, in the tangle of their lives, a private place where Rossetti's love affair with Morris's wife Janey could run its course. Janey and the Morris children would spend the summer there and Morris would come down by train for a few days at a time. He loved its quietness, the link with farming people of an earlier time, the beautiful garden, its closeness to the River Thames. Its weathered stone tugged at his heart.

The next invaders were American artists, and only slightly related to the Arts and Crafts movement, but they are important in this story because they 'discovered' Broadway. Edwin Abbey was a small, genial painter and illustrator who liked to draw scenes of 18th-century bourgeois life. Frank Millet had been an art student, a soldier and a journalist, and was hoping to settle down to painting historical

Kelmscott Manor, a bird's-eye view by Edmund Hort New
(Courtesy of the Society of Antiquaries)

The Green at Broadway in about 1900, with Farnham House on the left, photographed by Henry Taunt
(Courtesy of the National Monuments Record)

scenes in oils. They were used to scouring the countryside for settings for their work. In the summer of 1884 Millet visited Broadway. What he saw was one long street lined with cottages, farmhouses and some grander houses, sitting under the edge of the Cotswold escarpment. In earlier times it had been an important staging post on the road from London to Worcester, but it was less prosperous now, for the railway had bypassed it. It was exactly what he and Abbey wanted, a countryside full of historical and literary associations. They felt they were in Shakespeare's country. Millet decided that the following year he would take Farnham House, by the village green, as a summer house with his wife and children.

When they came the next year, Abbey and Millet brought their literary and artistic friends with them, including the writer Henry James and the painter John Singer Sargent, who painted his well-known *Carnation, Lily, Lily, Rose* in Broadway, under the influence of Impressionism. They were all on holiday and there was much skylarking in the street; the villagers just said 'them Americans is out again'.[2] They came back again in the summer of 1886, only this year instead of Farnham House they took Russell House, about two hundred metres down the road to Evesham, which had a barn adjoining which could be used as a studio. The floor was levelled, and Abbey brought down all his props, furniture and musical instruments from London. There was also a ruined grange or manor house standing not far from Russell House, built in the 14th century by the monks of Pershore. Its ramshackle Gothic spaces also became studios and writing rooms. By now there was a rhythm to their Bohemian days. They worked in the morning, played tennis in the afternoon, and in the evening they would have supper and games, such games, in the big barn-studio: palm reading, poker, dressing up in Abbey's wealth of props. One day they all went out rowing down the Avon, with Abbey playing the banjo and Henry James sitting like Buddha in the prow of the boat. A few years later, James published an enthusiastic article about Broadway in *Harper's New Monthly Magazine* which, as Abbey remarked, 'did not much help the privacy of the place.' [3]

These summer painting parties came to an end in 1889. In 1890 Abbey and Sargent took another Cotswold house, Morgan Hall at Fairford, where they painted the murals for the public library at Boston, Massachusetts. The Millets settled into Russell House as their summer home, and wintered each year in New York. Millet owned the house, and the ruined grange had been bequeathed to him by its owner, so he set about repairing it with great enthusiasm. Sargent said he wished Millet would do more painting and less plumbing. He used the building

Abbot's Grange,
a pen drawing by Edmund Hort
New, published in
The Quest 1 (1894-5), p. 10

THE·GRANGE·BROAD·
WAY·FROM·THE·WEST

Abbot's Grange from the west, 1978

as a backdrop for his history paintings, and added a studio wing at the north end in 1907, designed by the Arts and Crafts architect Andrew Prentice. Then, on the night of 16 April 1912, he was drowned on the *Titanic*.

The grange passed to his widow Lily who knew as much about these things as he did – when her children had grown up she started an interior decorating business in New York. In her hands it became a home again. With Prentice's help she altered the studio to a drawing room with bedrooms above and added a wing to the south-west corner of the old house. Abbot's Grange, as it became known, was probably sold in 1923, and ten years later a north wing was added, designed by C. E. Bateman, one of the leading Arts and Crafts architects from Birmingham. Both Prentice's and Bateman's wings demonstrate their respect for old work: they sympathise in style with the medieval core but are carefully grouped to stand a little apart from it, as if cradling the house's monkish past.

(Abbot's Grange is not included in the Broadway walks because you cannot see it without encroaching on the owners' privacy.)

Part of Orchard Farm, Broadway, sketched by Charles Rennie Mackintosh, September 1894
(Courtesy of the Hunterian Art Gallery, University of Glasgow)

The painters came first, then the architects. It is surprising they did not come before, for the Cotswold stone farmhouses and yeomen's houses were perfect models for the middle-class houses which late-Victorian architects loved to build. And the simplicity and regional character of Cotswolds buildings appealed to the Arts and Crafts architects among them. But until the late 1880s architects only knew about Cotswold churches. A young London architect called Guy Dawber told them about the houses. In 1887 he got a job as clerk of works on the building of Batsford Park, near Moreton-in-Marsh, because office work hurt his eyes. In 1888 he wrote an article about Broadway praising its picturesqueness. In 1893 he wrote more soberly, marrying the Cotswold building tradition to Arts and Crafts tastes. Its great merits, he said, were simplicity and restraint, 'a breadth of treatment and grasp of composition almost unknown today.'[4] Dawber was showing what progressive architects wanted to see. Young architects came to sketch; Charles Rennie Mackintosh from Glasgow was one of them, the following year. Soon a stone-built neo-vernacular became almost the common language of 20th-century building in the Cotswolds.

In 1893 three young architects, Ernest Gimson and the brothers Ernest and
Sidney Barnsley, settled in the south Cotswolds, near Cirencester. All three had
worked in London offices, but it was the office side of architecture they disliked.
They wanted to work at domestic crafts and get their hands dirty with building.
The Cotswolds seemed to be the place to do it. Ernest Barnsley was jolly and
sociable, but there was a lonely, spiritual side to Gimson and Sidney Barnsley
which relished the hidden Cotswold valleys. Sidney Barnsley designed and made
furniture, working entirely on his own. Gimson designed furniture, metalwork and
plasterwork, briefly in partnership with Ernest Barnsley and then by himself. He
and Ernest Barnsley employed skilled cabinetmakers from London and elsewhere,
but their furniture, and Sidney Barnsley's, quotes unmistakably from country
woodwork: the curved rails at the back of the sideboard above derive from farm
wagons. So this was neither rural nor urban craftsmanship but a third thing: the
seed of urban craftsmanship planted in country soil.

Country life means different things to different people. Gimson was an enemy of
religious belief and found an austere satisfaction in the Cotswolds, keeping
company with the landscape. Mary Anderson was a devout Roman Catholic from
Kentucky who enjoyed great success on the London stage in the 1880s and married
a wealthy Spanish-American. She retired to Broadway in 1895, where she lived a
comfortable country life and kept company with her literary and artistic friends.
On coming to Broadway, Mary Anderson was surprised to find that she already
knew people in the neighbourhood: Mary Elcho at Stanway House, the heart of
the cultured circle of aristocrats known as 'the Souls'; Lord Redesdale with his
Japanese garden at Batsford Park; the Flower family, brewers of Stratford-on-Avon
and promoters of the Shakespeare Memorial Theatre. Arts and Crafts people who
thought they were discovering the Cotswolds found a sophisticated gentry and
aristocracy there already, moving back and forth by train between London and the
country.

Katie Adams did not strictly speaking come to the Cotswolds, for she was there already. Her father was vicar of Little Faringdon, near Kelmscott, and as a child she played with the Morris children. In her twenties she kept house for her father and mother. In 1897, when she was in her mid-thirties, she had to start earning her own living so she took bookbinding lessons and set up a workshop in Lechlade. In 1901, when her father was made rector of Weston-sub-Edge, she moved her workshop to nearby Broadway. Her clients included local people, and also a trio of outstanding Arts and Crafts bookmen in London: Emery Walker who advised William Morris on printing techniques, St John Hornby who ran his own private press, and Sydney Cockerell, scholar and collector. If one of these three wanted something special bound, he would send it to Broadway to be, as Cockerell put it, 'Katied'. She worked quietly and well, charged reasonable prices, was not ambitious except for the quality of her work, and generated much love among her friends. Emery Walker once told her that he wanted to see her recognised as the first artist binder in England.

What we have seen so far has amounted to little more than raiding parties on the Cotswolds, a couple of architects here, an artist there, a bookbinder. But in the summer of 1902 there was a real invasion: about 150 men, women and children descended on the little town of Chipping Campden. They were the craftsmen of C. R. Ashbee's Guild of Handicraft, their wives and children.

When the guild started in East London in 1888 it consisted of four workmen and Ashbee, an idealistic young architect. But by 1900 he had transformed it into a limited company with workshops for metalwork, furniture, jewellery, silversmithing, wrought-iron work and printing, employing about forty men. It was very much a London workshop, but in the late 1890s Ashbee began to think of moving it out into the country. He was thinking about health in cities, and he was also thinking, as Arts and Crafts people did, that perhaps the crafts belonged in the country.

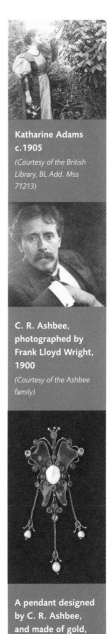

Katharine Adams c.1905
(Courtesy of the British Library, BL Add. Mss 71213)

C. R. Ashbee, photographed by Frank Lloyd Wright, 1900
(Courtesy of the Ashbee family)

A pendant designed by C. R. Ashbee, and made of gold, enamel, garnets, amethysts and pearls. c. 1899
(Private collection)

He looked at several possible sites, and probably chose Campden because there was an empty silk mill which could accommodate his workshops and because of the astonishing beauty of the High Street. Here, as in Broadway, Cotswold-stone houses lined the main street. But if Broadway was a big village, Campden was a small town. It was off the beaten track, but it had urbanity. The 16th-, 17th- and 18th-century houses in the High Street were those of a prosperous country town, and over them all stood the 15th-century tower of the parish church, built when Campden was made rich by the sale of Cotswold wool. As Ashbee walked down the High Street, he could relish these former glories. But he also saw houses standing empty and neglected. 'This is the nineteenth century,' he would think, 'the great industrial cities are draining the countryside.' Standing at the beginning of the twentieth century, he could see his workshops reversing that trend, bringing life back.

The workshops went into the silk mill in Sheep Street; there were cottages available for married guildsmen; and Ashbee and his wife Janet moved into a

Four guildsmen
in Sheep Street,
Chipping Campden
(Courtesy of the Cameron
family)

partly 14th-century house in the High Street. In what now seems the most typically romantic episode of the Arts and Crafts movement in England, Ashbee and his Cockney guildsmen were crowning their East End achievements by marrying past and present, town and country, easing themselves back into history and at the same time bringing new life to a little country town. Ashbee was a man of extraordinary energy, always eager to make the world a better place; town or country, it did not matter to him. The Campden children looked unhealthy, so he built a swimming pool. He revived the town band and put on plays in the Town Hall. Finding that shirts went to Evesham to be starched, he set up the Campden School of Arts and Crafts, teaching cookery, laundry and gardening alongside crafts. Journalists came and wrote admiring articles. With each returning spring, it seemed as if a workshop paradise had been created.

For the people of Campden, though, there were difficulties. It was not easy for a community of about 1750 people to absorb about 150 newcomers. And housing caused bad feelings: the cottages were empty for guildsmen because the landlord had turned out farming tenants to make way for them. And then there was the almost arrogant speed with which Ashbee moved, as if Campden was a kind of Sleeping Beauty and he was the prince. Campden was not asleep. Many of 'his' improvements – the band, the swimming pool, technical education – were in hand before the guild arrived. But he moved so fast he did not have time to notice that he was not the only progressive person in the town.

The workshop paradise was sadly short-lived. In 1905 the guild began to make a loss. A business manager was appointed in 1906, but things had gone too far, and in 1908 the Guild of Handicraft Limited went into liquidation. For most of Ashbee's forty or so workmen, liquidation meant going back to the big cities and searching for work. Arthur Cameron, a cocky young Londoner whom Ashbee had helped to become a skilful enameller, went back to London but could not find work, and spent two years sleeping rough, his wife and children in the workhouse. 'The collapse of the Guild' his son wrote later, 'was <u>his</u> collapse too.' [5]

Liquidation in 1908 brought Ashbee's project almost to an end. But in Campden it also created a beginning, for some of the ablest guildsmen stayed on, working under their own names in the silk mill. The cabinetmaker Jim Pyment started a building and cabinetmaking firm which earned a reputation for the skilful repair of old buildings; the firm still exists. Alec Miller, the most intellectual of the guildsmen (the most like Ashbee) set up as a carver and sculptor and worked in Campden until the late 1930s, when he emigrated to California. Bill Thornton and Charley Downer, the guild blacksmiths, worked together until the Second World War, maintaining, Miller wrote, 'that atmosphere of truculent silence for which the forge was always known.'[6] The silversmith George Hart made his name in 1926 when his design for the Royal Ascot Hunt Cup won a competition organised by the Goldsmiths' Company, and since then work has been continuous at Hart Silversmiths. George's son Henry joined him in the 1930s and Henry's son David in the 1950s, and civic, church and presentation silver has been one of their strengths. George Hart died in 1973 and Henry in 1990.

Alec Miller, photographed by Jesse Taylor in about 1910
(Courtesy of the Guild of Handicraft Trust)

The workshop is currently in David Hart's hands, but he expects to retire soon, and will hand it on to his son William, his nephew Julian, and Derek Elliot, who trained with him. This year the workshop celebrates a hundred years of silversmithing in the silk mill.

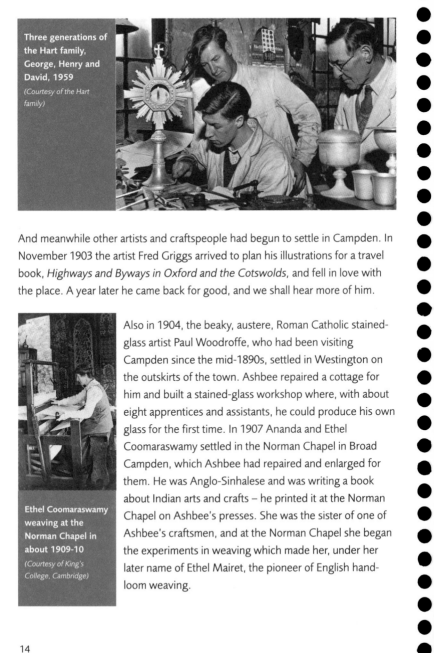

Three generations of the Hart family, George, Henry and David, 1959

(Courtesy of the Hart family)

And meanwhile other artists and craftspeople had begun to settle in Campden. In November 1903 the artist Fred Griggs arrived to plan his illustrations for a travel book, *Highways and Byways in Oxford and the Cotswolds,* and fell in love with the place. A year later he came back for good, and we shall hear more of him.

Ethel Coomaraswamy weaving at the Norman Chapel in about 1909-10

(Courtesy of King's College, Cambridge)

Also in 1904, the beaky, austere, Roman Catholic stained-glass artist Paul Woodroffe, who had been visiting Campden since the mid-1890s, settled in Westington on the outskirts of the town. Ashbee repaired a cottage for him and built a stained-glass workshop where, with about eight apprentices and assistants, he could produce his own glass for the first time. In 1907 Ananda and Ethel Coomaraswamy settled in the Norman Chapel in Broad Campden, which Ashbee had repaired and enlarged for them. He was Anglo-Sinhalese and was writing a book about Indian arts and crafts – he printed it at the Norman Chapel on Ashbee's presses. She was the sister of one of Ashbee's craftsmen, and at the Norman Chapel she began the experiments in weaving which made her, under her later name of Ethel Mairet, the pioneer of English hand-loom weaving.

In Broadway at this time there was a teenager who was coming under the spell of the Arts and Crafts, learning about furniture, watching builders make stone walls. His name was Gordon Russell and he came to Broadway in 1904 after his father had bought the Lygon Arms to turn it into an hotel. In about 1907 his father started a small antiques business and Gordon worked in the furniture-repair shop

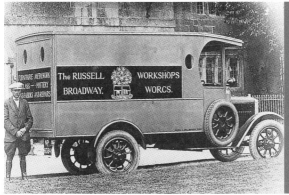

A Russell Workshops van, late 1920s. The cottage emblem was designed by Paul Woodroffe.
(Courtesy of the Gordon Russell Trust)

attached to it. In 1919 he joined his father running Russell & Sons, which not only sold and repaired antiques, but also made new furniture. As the new furniture business expanded, it was renamed Russell Workshops in 1927 and Gordon Russell Ltd in 1929. The craftsmen worked in beautifully restored old buildings near the Lygon Arms and produced individual pieces to Gordon Russell's designs, which owed a lot to the work of Ernest Gimson and Sidney Barnsley. This was all in the spirit of the Arts and Crafts, though most Arts and Crafts people were not such natural salesmen as the Russells. But there was one point of difference: machinery. Gordon Russell liked mechanical things and saw machines as complex tools. Arts and Crafts people mostly felt that machinery had already destroyed traditions of craftsmanship and made work soulless. Here was a divide.

During the 1920s he gradually introduced new machinery which could produce standard designs in batches. In 1929 his brother Dick, who worked in a more modern style, took over the designing, and Russell himself was able to give more time to writing and lecturing, urging his undogmatic but unchanging belief that the values of the Arts and Crafts, its sense of materials and workmanship, should be brought to bear on the larger world of industry. These ideas were of the time. During and after the Second World War he was involved in the government's Utility scheme for standardised, inexpensive furniture, and from 1947 to 1959 he was director of the Council of Industrial Design, later the Design Council. For two decades, at the height of his career, his weekdays were spent in London. Thus, in this little story of Arts and Crafts in the Cotswolds, Gordon Russell holds a peculiar place, for he was going in the opposite direction from everybody else, from the Cotswolds to London.

The story of Gordon Russell has taken us beyond the First World War, beyond the high flourishing time of the Arts and Crafts movement. But the war was not altogether a time of ending for the crafts, and in the Cotswolds workshops and artist-craftsmen were, if anything, thicker on the ground on the 1920s and 1930s than they had been earlier. If the invasion of the Cotswolds took place at the turn of the century, the period between the wars was a time of settlement. In this rich landscape the arts and crafts flourished in great numbers. Too great for the scope of this essay: all I can do is skim over the landscape, noting some of the principal figures and workshops, ignoring others.

In the south, Ernest Gimson died in 1919 and Ernest and Sidney Barnsley in 1926. But in a triangle between Sapperton, Stroud and Painswick there were: the architect Norman Jewson; Louise Powell, calligrapher and pottery painter, and her husband Alfred, architect and pottery painter; William Simmonds, sculptor and puppetmaster; Peter Waals, cabinetmaker, who had been Gimson's foreman and carried on that tradition of furniture-making at Chalford until he died in 1937;

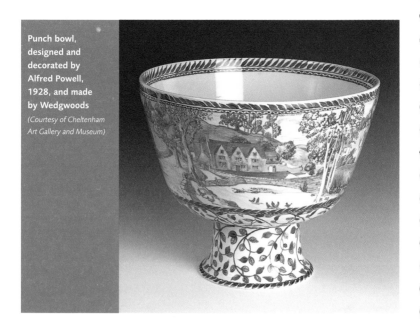

Punch bowl, designed and decorated by Alfred Powell, 1928, and made by Wedgwoods
(Courtesy of Cheltenham Art Gallery and Museum)

Henry Payne, stained-glass artist, Charles March Gere, painter, and Mary Newill, embroideress and stained-glass artist, all three of whom had earlier worked in Birmingham; and the textile artists Phyllis Barron and Dorothy Larcher, the leading hand-block printers of the time. (These last four lived in Painswick, where there were enough Arts and Crafts people to share a subscription to the *Burlington Magazine*, then the only English journal of art history and connoisseurship.)

Detail of the west window, Our Lady and St Peter's Roman Catholic Church, Leatherhead, Surrey, by Paul Woodroffe, 1924
(Photograph by Peter Cormack)

F. L. Griggs, *Owlpen Manor,* **etching, 1931**

Further north, the potter Michael Cardew took over a country pottery at Winchcombe in 1926, hoping to emulate the ordinariness of the pottery's earlier products – flower pots, milk pans, chimney pots. People who bought Cardew's pots were not supposed to mind when they got broken. There was not much craft activity in Broadway between the wars apart from the the weaver Dennis Baker, a pupil of Ethel Mairet, and the Russell firm. But in Chipping Campden there were the former guildsmen working in the silk mill; Paul Woodroffe, who worked in Campden until 1934; F. L. Griggs; the ex-Birmingham craftspeople Arthur and Georgie Gaskin and Bernard Sleigh; newcomers like H. P. R. Finberg's Alcuin Press and the Kingsley Weavers. Ashbee had left in 1919 but there were enough artist-craftsmen here to furnish substantial exhibitions organised by the Campden Society in the 1920s and 1930s.

Griggs was the principal Arts and Crafts figure in Campden between the wars. He led the artists of the town, and had a kind of historical sadness on him. He talked of 'England' as something almost lost. 'England' was the beauty of the fields and hills mingled with regret for an earlier, more organic state of society. He came from a Baptist family but in 1912 he became a Catholic and found a kind of fixedness in that. At about the same time he began work on the series of etchings of real and imagined Gothic buildings, many of them ruined, which made his reputation and occupied him until his death. He loved the Gothic stonework that he drew so credibly, and saw in it a beauty and a holiness that stood outside time. But he knew that you cannot stand outside time. Here, again, was loss.

The etchings were a private part of Griggs's imagination; Campden was a public part. Its beauty was part of what he meant by 'England' and he could not bear much change in the town. He planned but never completed a book of writings about Campden, illustrated by wood engravings of his own drawings, that would at least preserve his vision of the place. (Some of the wood engravings were published after his death.) And he began to intervene in the public life and fabric of Campden. In 1919 he made a sketch for a war memorial by the Town Hall and for some months the town argued about it. Some people thought Griggs was not

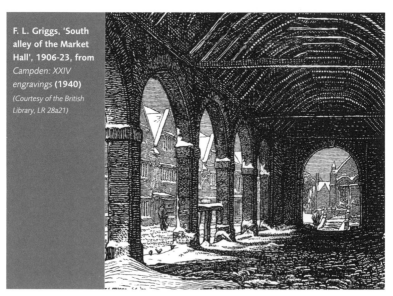

F. L. Griggs, 'South alley of the Market Hall', 1906-23, from *Campden: XXIV engravings* **(1940)**
(Courtesy of the British Library, LR 28a21)

suited to the work because he had not fought in the war (there was also, perhaps, a hint of anti-Catholicism). Others supported his design, including Paul Woodroffe, Alec Miller and Wentworth Huyshe, all artist-craftsmen. In October an angry meeting was held in the town hall at which the anti-Griggs party was routed with cries of 'Bloody liar!' from the floor. The memorial stands today, remembering the dead, and forgetting the anger of those who opposed it.

F. L. Griggs (right), with George Chettle, architect, Hilda Pook, Ashbee's secretary, and Alec Miller, c. 1908.
(Courtesy of the Guild of Handicraft Trust)

Throughout the 1920s, Griggs worked to safeguard the fabric that he loved. In 1924 he was the moving spirit in the establishment of the Campden Society to protect the character of the town and promote its arts and crafts. In 1926 Dover's Hill, a favourite walking spot and site of the traditional Dover's Games to the west of the town, was advertised for sale as an ideal site for an hotel. There was no time to raise the necessary money by subscription, so Griggs bought it himself and paid heavy interest on his overdraft for the next two years, until it was transferred to the National Trust. In 1929 he set up the Campden Trust, which intervened more directly by buying up historic buildings, restoring them and selling them on. Nowadays, when Griggs and his contemporaries are dead and only the fabric that he saved remains, his work seems admirable, uncontroversial. But in the 1920s there was hostility towards him in the town, as keeping himself to himself too much. And one can see how exclusively aesthetic his love of Campden was. He wanted to save the Campden of his imagination, a place he loved best when no one was around, walking on Dover's Hill at dawn, sitting in his studio at night, listening to the bells of the parish church. Church bells moved him more than anything. There was not enough room in his fiercely anti-modern imagination for the people of Campden as they lived in the 1920s and 1930s. If the town had been empty, he might have loved it even more.

When he first came to Campden, Griggs stayed at Braithwaite House with the young men of the Guild of Handicraft. Then, in 1906, he leased the beautiful 18th-century Dovers House, a few doors away in the High Street. He continued to live there after he married in 1922. As his family grew, he began to think of building a house for himself, a project that was heavy, not only with the romantic meanings of his etchings, but also with his increasingly mixed feelings about Campden. In 1926 he bought land behind Leysbourne, stretching back towards Dover's Hill, and a year later designed a U-shaped building, a studio in one wing,

Griggs's house under construction, in about May 1930

(Courtesy of the Guild of Handicraft Trust)

most of the family accommodation in the middle, and a drawing room in the other with a long library over it, in which his soul could dwell. It looked over the roofs of Campden towards the parish church, but it was hidden from Campden's eyes, only reached through a door in the terrace on the north side of Leysbourne.

When he started he perhaps could afford to build such a house, for he was making a tolerable income from his etchings and he planned to build slowly. Work began in 1927 and the house is remarkable, not just for its design but also for the way it was built, the deliberate use of English materials that were stronger, better, heavier, bigger than the work demanded, as if to outface time. The builder said deal would do for that beam, so Griggs used oak. He wanted dressed stonework in the cellar, and the builder objected that no one would see it. Griggs said it was good for the builders to know it was there.

Griggs's house in 2002. It is now known as Dovers Court.
(Photograph by John Williams)

In 1929 Wall Street crashed and as a minor consequence the bottom fell out of the etchings market. Griggs's income fell disastrously. The studio wing was then finished, and the family range was in progress. He could have changed the design and settled for a smaller house. But he went on building. In 1930 he was forced to move into the unfinished house, but the builder would not make the house ready until he was paid. So Griggs arranged to hand over his collection of his own etchings to a friendly patron for £750, on the understanding that he could buy it back when he had the money. He never did. When the Griggs family moved, early in October, they were without outside doors, and had no doors to the room they ate in. The house was structurally complete, but work on the interior progressed only gradually. In 1933 he raised more money by selling his treasured collection of Turner etchings, but it was not enough. He died in 1938, encumbered with debt, and with the house still not quite finished.

He had always called it 'The Ruins', or sometimes 'Griggs's Folly'. Both names referred affectionately to the world of his etchings, but both must have become steadily more bitter to him through the years, especially when he thought of the wife and children who would survive him.

(Griggs's house still stands in Back Ends, though it was damaged by fire in the early 1970s. Please note that it is a private house, and not open to the public).

The Arts and Crafts movement did not end at any particular time in the Cotswolds, or anywhere else for that matter, but Griggs's house can perhaps be taken for its swansong in this part of the country. C. R. Ashbee thought it was 'probably the most beautiful modern house in England.' [7]

1 Quoted in David Verey, *The buildings of England: Gloucestershire 1: The Cotswolds* (1970), p. 53

2 Stanley Olson, Warren Adelson and Richard Ormond, *Sargent at Broadway: The Impressionist years* (1986), p. 19

3 Quoted in E. V. Lucas, *Edwin Austin Abbey*, 2 vols, (1921), vol. 1, p. 148

4 *Builder* 20 May 1893, p. 387

5 Ashbee Journals, King's College, Cambridge, 26 June 1939

6 Ashbee Journals, 27 March 1921

7 Letter to Griggs, 24 July 1936, Griggs family archive

Broadway

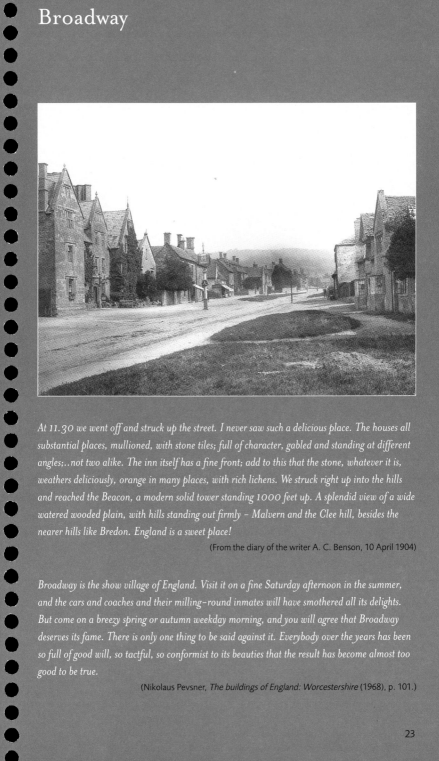

At 11.30 we went off and struck up the street. I never saw such a delicious place. The houses all substantial places, mullioned, with stone tiles; full of character, gabled and standing at different angles;..not two alike. The inn itself has a fine front; add to this that the stone, whatever it is, weathers deliciously, orange in many places, with rich lichens. We struck right up into the hills and reached the Beacon, a modern solid tower standing 1000 feet up. A splendid view of a wide watered wooded plain, with hills standing out firmly – Malvern and the Clee hill, besides the nearer hills like Bredon. England is a sweet place!

(From the diary of the writer A. C. Benson, 10 April 1904)

Broadway is the show village of England. Visit it on a fine Saturday afternoon in the summer, and the cars and coaches and their milling-round inmates will have smothered all its delights. But come on a breezy spring or autumn weekday morning, and you will agree that Broadway deserves its fame. There is only one thing to be said against it. Everybody over the years has been so full of good will, so tactful, so conformist to its beauties that the result has become almost too good to be true.

(Nikolaus Pevsner, *The buildings of England: Worcestershire* (1968), p. 101.)

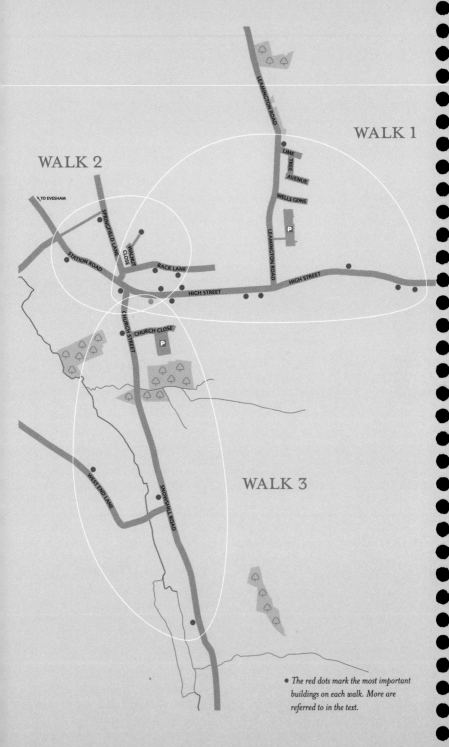

WALK 1

WALK 2

WALK 3

TO EVESHAM

LEAMINGTON ROAD

LIME
TREE
AVENUE

WELLS GDNS

LEAMINGTON ROAD

P

SPRINGFIELD LANE

WALNUT
CLOSE

STATION ROAD

BACK LANE

HIGH STREET

HIGH STREET

CHURCH STREET

CHURCH CLOSE

P

WEST END LANE

SNOWSHILL ROAD

• The red dots mark the most important
buildings on each walk. More are
referred to in the text.

Planning your walks

Broadway caters for tourists who come by car or coach. There is a large car park in the angle of the High Street and Church Street, with prize-winning public loos. This car park is convenient for the War Memorial from which all three walks start, and there is another in Leamington Road. To judge distances, see the scale on the maps that accompany each walk.

On **Walk 1: The High Street and Leamington Road**, you follow the same route as other tourists, walking from west to east up the High Street which made Broadway famous, exploring the interventions which Arts and Crafts architects made in the fabric of the village. It is a longish walk with an optional detour in the middle down Leamington Road, and there are buildings at either end of it which are important in the story: the Lygon Arms in the west, run by Gordon Russell's father, and Court Farm in the east, the home of the famous American actress, Mary Anderson.

Walk 2: The Green, Station Road, Springfield Lane and Back Lane, is more of an exploration. It has the feeling of getting round the back of things. It starts with two houses connected with the American artists who first came to Broadway in the 1880s, Farnham House and Russell House; then it turns up a little bridlepath into Springfield Lane which has a slightly suburban air; and then it goes down Back Lane behind the High Street, to explore the site of the former Gordon Russell furniture factory and the back buildings of the Lygon Arms.

Walk 3: Church Street, Snowshill Road and West End Lane, goes along Church Street and Snowshill Road as far as the church of St Eadburga, which was the medieval parish church of Broadway. It is a walk in the country, which in good weather can be very beautiful, and it is dotted with buildings skilfully repaired and enlarged by two of the principal architects of early 20th-century Broadway, C. E. Bateman and Guy Dawber. From the end of this walk you can easily walk back to Broadway across the fields.

The history of Broadway

It helps to think of the village map as shaped like an L. The long High Street is the stem and the foot is Church Street, running into Snowshill Road.

Medieval Broadway lay chiefly along the foot of the L, and the important surviving buildings of medieval Broadway are in Church Street and Snowshill Road. They are the church of St Eadburga, a mile and a quarter south of the green, which would have been the principal church of medieval Broadway, and Abbot's Grange in Church Street, which was a grange or manor of the Abbots of Pershore.

The High Street, on the other hand, is lined with houses which are, at least externally, mostly of 16th- to 19th-century date, and they reflect the prosperity of the village in post-medieval times. This was partly due to travellers and merchants, for Broadway lay on the old road from London to Worcester. It was the collective beauty of these houses which earned Broadway a reputation in the twentieth century as the show village of England.

That reputation was partly made by the artists, architects and craftspeople celebrated in these pages. To judge from old photographs, Broadway was not as trim in the late 19th century as it is today. Agricultural depression was probably one cause of this, the replacement of road transport by the railways another. Work began on the Oxford, Worcester and Wolverhampton Railway in 1845, but it completely bypassed Broadway, and a branch line was not opened until 1904. Noakes's *Guide to Worcestershire* for 1868 reported sadly that 'neither coach nor wagon finds its way through the village – at least but rarely.' This was the village to which artists and others came in the 1880s.

**A cottage in Church Street,
Broadway, 1894**
*(Photograph by Sir Benjamin Stone, courtesy
of Birmingham Reference Library)*

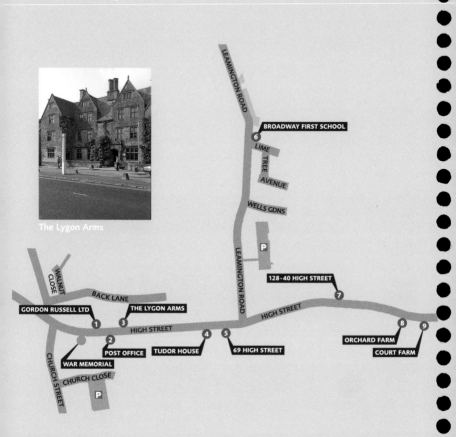

The Lygon Arms

LEAMINGTON ROAD

BROADWAY FIRST SCHOOL

6

LIME

TREE

AVENUE

WELLS GDNS

P

LEAMINGTON ROAD

128-40 HIGH STREET

7

WALNUT CLOSE

BACK LANE

GORDON RUSSELL LTD

1

3

THE LYGON ARMS

HIGH STREET

HIGH STREET

2

POST OFFICE

TUDOR HOUSE

4

5

69 HIGH STREET

8

ORCHARD FARM

9

COURT FARM

WAR MEMORIAL

CHURCH STREET

CHURCH CLOSE

P

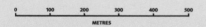

0   100   200   300   400   500

METRES

● *The red dots mark the most important buildings on each walk. More are referred to in the text.*

The High Street runs from west to east, so buildings are described here as on the north or south sides. This walk, like the others, starts from the

War Memorial erected just east of the green. It was designed c. 1922 by F. L. Griggs.

Standing by the memorial and looking across the road, you can see a building with a two-storey porch and small dormers; this and its neighbour on the right are the

Former offices and showroom of Gordon Russell Limited (1), furniture makers. The left-hand building was probably built in the late 17th century. Gordon Russell's father, S. B. Russell, bought it and added the porch in 1916, to designs by C. E. Bateman. After the war it became the showrooms of the Russell furniture firm, together with the handsome 18th-century house on the right. Until recently the showrooms were home to a fine historical collection of furniture from the workshops, mostly designed by Gordon Russell. But in 2001 the American company Steelcase Strafor, owners of the Russell firm, moved the workshops and offices to Worcester. The historical collection is now in the care of the Gordon Russell Trust, which hopes to find a home for them on the Broadway site.

Chest of drawers designed by Gordon Russell for David Lloyd George 1928
(Courtesy of the Gordon Russell Trust)

On the south side, by the traffic lights, is the

Post Office (2). This was built in 1899 and designed by Guy Dawber. Around 1900 the Post Office did not have its own architect's department, and its premises were usually designed by the government's Office of Works. The Post Office thought the results were often mean and characterless, and looked for opportunities to employ outside architects. In Broadway they employed the architect who had first drawn the Cotswold vernacular to the profession's attention, and were rewarded with a design which was both distinctive and in keeping with the High Street.

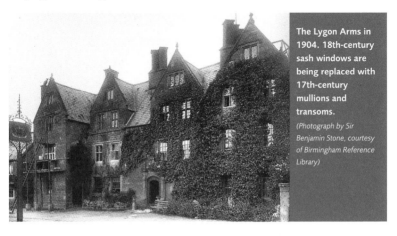

The Lygon Arms in 1904. 18th-century sash windows are being replaced with 17th-century mullions and transoms.
(Photograph by Sir Benjamin Stone, courtesy of Birmingham Reference Library)

If you stand with your back to the Post Office, on the north side is

The Lygon Arms (3). This is the finest house in Broadway, with a date of 1620 over the door. It was probably a private house at first and then became an inn. During the 18th century it was called The White Hart. Much of Broadway's prosperity derived from the hospitality which the Lygon Arms offered to travellers, but when Gordon Russell's father, Sydney Bolton Russell, bought it in 1903 he was intent on changing it from a substantial country inn into a first-rate hotel. He enjoyed stripping away Victorian and earlier accretions and 'putting back' its 17th-century character. The writer A. C. Benson described S. B. Russell as 'a nice landlord, a gentlemanly young man interested in antiquities – anxious to restore his house. He says it is full all the summer of Americans'.

As the Lygon prospered, he began to enlarge it. For instance, a large roughcast shed stood in a garden to the right of the building and was used each year for the

North Cotswold Hunt Ball. In 1910 Russell replaced this with the low east range which is now the great hall and dining room, a richly detailed design in the Cotswold idiom by C. E. Bateman, a talented Arts and Crafts architect from Birmingham, who did much good work in Broadway.

Other additions in the Arts and Crafts spirit were made at this time and in the 1920s, but they are at the back of the hotel, and can be seen most easily from Back Lane, which is part of Walk 2 (see p. 43).

Tudor House, an architect's sketch, published in *The Builder*, **1906**

Standing with your back to the Lygon Arms, you can see, on the south side, **Lloyd's Bank,** *originally the Capital and Counties Bank, designed in 1914 by a local architect, George Henry Hunt who worked with C. E. Bateman. Compare the breadth and simplicity of this building with the dry, stiff handling of the Cotswold idiom in the HSBC Bank further up the High Street, designed in 1921 by the Liverpool architects Woolfall and Eccles.*

Now walk up the north side of the road. This will bring you to a sudden gap in the houses on the south side, through which there is a beautiful open view across the fields towards Broadway Hill. For much of its length on this side, the High Street is only lined with single houses which enjoy this view from their gardens. Pause in front of the Horse and Hound pub. Then if you look across to the south side you will see

Tudor House (4), a 17th-century house, almost as fine as the Lygon Arms, repaired and altered by the Bedford architect, C. E. Mallows, for an American, Ben Chandler, in about 1909. Mallows was a talented architect in his own right but was better known as a draughtsman: his seductive perspective drawings, done in very soft Koh-i-Noor pencil on handmade paper, won many competitions for other architects. At Tudor House he worked in the spirit of the Arts and Crafts, doing as little to the house as he could, taking out old partitions, designing a new staircase on the old lines, and making a service wing which you see on the right, out of an early 19th-century stable block. The big shallow arch gave access to a garage, for Chandler owned a car. The worm was thus early in the bud.

Here is F. L. Griggs, who hated modern civilisation, writing to a friend in 1923 about Chandler who 'insisted on motoring us (in his silent and very fast car) to Stow, Burford, Northleach, the Coln Valley villages, Fairford, Lechlade, & home by Northleach & Stow. The whole round, including halts for visits to churches, to see views, to take in petrol, & for a picnic tea, took six hours!!! I never want to get in a car again. It seems like jeering at those dear places. The distances once were mysterious, & had their importance; we lose more than we gain in annihilating them it seems to me... What would it have been like to have walked down that Coln Valley from Foss Bridge to Fairford, with you, taking a day to do it!!'

The house next to Tudor House was called
'Eadburgha', after the saint to whom the old parish
church of Broadway is dedicated. In 1901, when the
Arts and Crafts bookbinder Katharine Adams moved
to Broadway, she set up in this house and worked
there until 1907, when she moved her workshop into
the white-plastered building with a many-paned
window on the other side of St Michael's School:

69 High Street (5). Katharine Adams started bookbinding in Lechlade in 1898, but when her clergyman father was made rector of Weston-sub-Edge in 1901, she moved her workshop to Broadway, bicycling the three miles to work so punctually that Weston people set their clocks by her. She had two helpers, Georgina Hampshire whom Gordon Russell remembered as 'a young woman with a bun of yellow hair, hand-woven clothes and sandals', and Jessie Gregory, who did the sewing, and they all worked in a big room behind the long window. There used to be a stained-glass window in the bindery, of an angel binding a book, by the Arts and Crafts stained-glass artist Christopher Whall.

Katie Adams usually bound in leather, decorating it in gold with little stamping tools of flowers, leaves and dots, filling the panels or compartments of her designs with simple central motifs or lacelike overall patterns. Though much of her work was for book collectors in London and elsewhere, she also did work for local people: prayer books for Mary de Navarro, *Country Life* for people in the big houses, a visitors' book for the Lygon Arms. In 1913, at the age of fifty-one, she married Edmund Webb, a gentleman astronomer, and in 1915 they went to live near Oxford. Her best work had been done in Broadway.

Continuing up the High Street, you come almost
immediately to Leamington Road. If you are feeling

energetic, you can make a detour down this road. On the right, after 300 metres, are four blocks of well-designed workers' cottages: **17-27 and 45-51 Leamington Road, and 1-7 and 2-8 Wells Gardens,** *of 1907-8, designed by George Henry Hunt (or perhaps C. E. Bateman for Hunt) for T. E. Wells, an American who lived in Broadway.*

Continue along Leamington Road for about 100 metres and you will come to

Broadway First School (6) of 1914, a simple and dignified design by C. E. Bateman. It is built of brick covered with render, with stone details and a slate roof. Cotswold stone would presumably have been too expensive for this building, and was perhaps not called for away from the High Street. Rendered brick was felt to be an unassuming and acceptable substitute.

Emery Walker, *A brief history of printing* **(1911), bound by Katharine Adams** *(Courtesy of Cheltenham Art Gallery and Museums)*

From here, return to the High Street. Exploring Broadway becomes more enjoyable at this point, since the building of a bypass has allowed the top of the High Street to be closed off, making it much quieter.

128-40 High Street, photographed by Francis Frith in 1899
(Courtesy of the Francis Frith Collection)

After about 250 metres, on the north side, are

128-40 High Street (7), the most sketched and photographed buildings in Broadway. They were popular with tourists, partly because of their beautiful position in the curve of the road underneath Broadway Hill, and partly because they were more like the popular image of a country cottage. The stone-built yeomen's houses that so pleased William Morris and Arts and Crafts architects suited a more specialised, not to say grander, taste. The photograph shows them in 1899. 138 was given its present form in 1938 by Espleys, a local building firm; and in 1942 Stewards, another local firm, carried out alterations to 140.

*At this point in the High Street, if you look towards the south-east, you get a good view of **Broadway Tower** up on the horizon. It was built by the Earl of Coventry in 1800 and has astounding views. In the 1870s it was rented by William Morris's friend, Cormell Price, and in 1876 Morris stayed there 'among the winds and clouds', as he wrote.*

*Set back, immediately after 128-40 High Street, is Fencote House, **144 High Street**, designed in 1936 by C. E. Bateman, for C. Steward, builder. Then we continue, between substantial 17th-century houses, for another 250 metres until we come on the south side to a group of former farm buildings which were turned into two of Broadway's most substantial turn-of-the-century houses. First,*

Orchard Farm (8). To make sense of the early history of the house, you need to stand in front of it: the parts to the right of the front door and behind the gable on the right were built in about 1620. Then, about a hundred years later, the part to the left of the front door was built, together with a barn which extended the house behind the gable on the right.

To make sense of the later history, you need to go back until you are in front of the gate. In 1905 the house was bought by Lady Maud Bowes Lyon, an aunt of the late Queen Mother, and her mother, the Countess of Strathmore. They had it repaired and enlarged by Andrew Prentice. He added a low kitchen wing at the east end, and altered the barn, raising its roof to create a music room with bedrooms above. The garden was divided up with topiary and dry-stone walls into separate 'rooms', a favourite ploy of architect-garden designers. The bird's-eye view gives a sense of how he envisaged it.

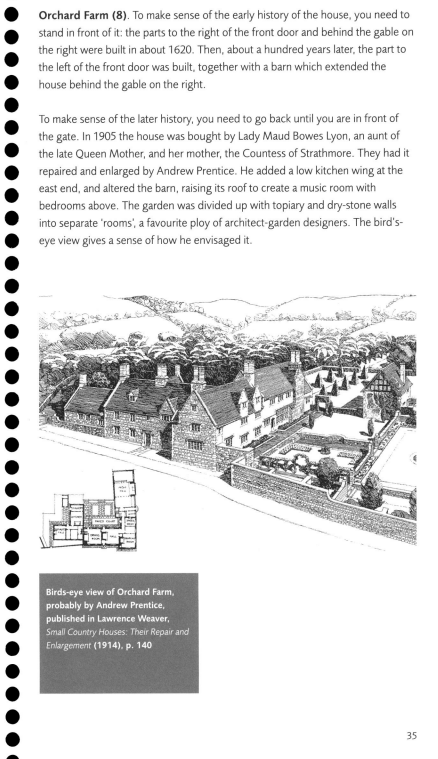

Birds-eye view of Orchard Farm, probably by Andrew Prentice, published in Lawrence Weaver, *Small Country Houses: Their Repair and Enlargement* **(1914), p. 140**

Court Farm, the garden front of the house in 1939. This part was originally Bell Farm.
(Courtesy of the Birmingham Post and Mail)

Then, past two smaller houses, we come to what looks like several houses partly set back behind low walls, but is in fact

Court Farm (9). It looks like several houses because it actually was two 17th-century farmhouses originally. On the right as you face them was Bell Farm, and on the left Court Farm. The gap between them came just east of the wing in the middle which reaches out to the road. In 1895 they were 'discovered' by the famous American actress Mary Anderson, recently married to Antonio de Navarro, and her friend, the composer Maude Valerie White, best known for her setting of Byron's 'So we'll go no more a roving'.

Mary Anderson describes their excitement:

'We ... found exactly what we wanted: two genuine Jacobean farmhouses at the foot of Broadway hill. One of these I specially liked, a picturesque old house, with pigsties and barns for a garden. I brought Tony to see it. He declared it a "bogey hole", and thought it could never be made habitable. I believed it could be made delightful....

'Maude took the house next to this. Hers was known as "Bell Farm", ours as "Court Farm". Our amusement now began. We discovered oak panelling, invisible inglenooks behind modern fireplaces, heavy oak beams and lovely little windows which had been hidden for centuries.'

When Maude Valerie White left Bell Farm to live in Sicily in about 1900, the de Navarros took over her house and employed Andrew Prentice to join the two together. He linked the two buildings with a large music room on the garden front, and there have been few alterations since, apart from a little flat-roofed wing at the east end of 1928 to house Antonio de Navarro's pewter collection, now in the Fitzwilliam Museum. From the road you can see that one of the dormer windows has stained glass in it. This lights a tiny chapel, and the glass was designed by Paul Woodroffe.

The garden was laid out by Alfred Parsons, artist and garden designer, in 1896 and then enlarged to take in that of Bell Farm. There is a paved area near the house, then large sweeping lawns, occasionally stepped, a very strong accent in some massive yew hedges to the west, and a note of formality in the rose garden. The whole lies against the backdrop of Broadway hill, on which the light does wonderful things. If much of the garden does not seem particularly 'designed', it is partly because Parsons treated the garden informally, as Gertrude Jekyll would have done, and such treatment became the norm for upper-middle-class gardens in England in the twentieth century.

WALK 2: The Green, Station Road, Springfield Lane and Back Lane

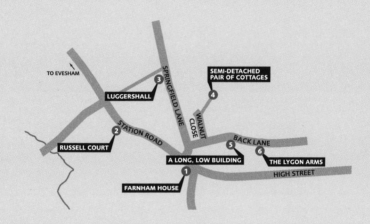

Luggershall

0   100   200   300   400   500

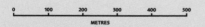

METRES

● *The red dots mark the most important buildings on each walk. More are referred to in the text.*

Starting from the War Memorial, walk down past the green until you are level with the Swan Inn. In front of you is

Farnham House (1) with its two big dormers in the roof. This is the house which was occupied by the American artist Frank Millet, his family and his friend Edwin Abbey during the summer of 1885, when they had first 'discovered' Broadway.

Cross Church Street and leave Farnham House on your left. Opposite the bus stop, behind a beech hedge, is **Cotswold Cottage**, *designed by Norman Jewson in 1930. Its pretty details, glimpsed above the hedge, are like someone quoting poetry in the next room. Then cross the road to get a full view of the* **Lifford Memorial Hall**, *a grand village hall of 1915 with a long roof and three gabled bays. It was designed by Andrew Prentice, who had worked for the Millets at Abbot's Grange and the de Navarros at Court Farm.*

Now continue down Station Road. After about 100 metres there is an 18th-century house with white-painted bay windows on the left. This is

Russell Court (2). Continue past the house as far as the drive and then look back. At the far left you see a gazebo looking out over the road (in the 19th century this was the first property in Broadway as you came from Evesham); then comes the main house, known as Russell House round 1900; then a lower, L-shaped range. The part nearest you, which runs back from the road, was originally a barn connected to the house by an arched range. The house was given much of its present form in the 1790s by the Russell family (no relation of Gordon Russell) and then in the late 19th and early 20th century by Frank Millet, the American artist.

This is the house which Millet and Abbey occupied during their second summer in Broadway, 1886. The barn was immediately turned into a studio. Later, Frank Millet acquired the house and it became his family's permanent summer residence. He also acquired, thanks to a bequest, the picturesque ruined grange, now called Abbot's Grange, standing near the green, which he repaired carefully and used as a studio; he then bought the meadows in between so that he could walk directly from one to the other. When he added a purpose-built studio to Abbot's Grange in 1907, the barn-studio at Russell House became a sitting room, hung with tapestries and filled with English and Dutch furniture of the 17th and 18th centuries. The room reflects both the family's own taste – Millet used such furniture in his history painting and Lily Millet sold it through the interior-decorating business she ran in New York – and the growing English taste for antiques. It is so typical of the making of the English past that it is easy to overlook its Americanness.

The sitting room at Russell House c. 1910
(Courtesy of Country Life Picture Library)

Shortly after Russell Court you will come to the Cheltenham Road. Turn right up the bridlepath opposite Cheltenham Road. This will give you glimpses, to your right, of

Luggershall (3) which you will see more fully when you turn right into Springfield Lane. The house was originally called Luggershill, and was built for Alfred Parsons, an English painter and one of the group of artists who 'discovered' Broadway in the mid-1880s. His paintings were of gardens or of intimate country scenes – rural England as a garden. Parsons was a bachelor and a busy and productive painter. For most of his career he lived in London, but in about 1911 he decided to retire to Broadway, partly to be near his old friend Frank Millet at Russell Court. He built Luggershill, designed by Andrew Prentice, but a kind of sadness hangs over the project, for the house was scarcely finished when Millet was drowned on the *Titanic*. Millet's last letter, mailed from Queenstown, Ireland, was to Parsons.

Parsons laid out his own garden at Luggershill and it was a comfort to him in his retirement. He died on 16 January 1920.

Continue down Springfield Lane, which comes out into the car park of the Swan Inn. But at that point you should turn sharp left into Back Lane. About 60 metres down Back Lane turn left into Walnut Close, and then follow the road out at the corner of the cul-de-sac. This will bring you to a

Semi-detached pair of cottages (4) designed by C. E. Bateman for the Russell furniture firm in 1924. Stone, with simple canopies over the door, thatch gently curving over the dormers and fat brick chimneys capped with stone. There were originally five other pairs, but they were burnt down.

Return to Back Lane, and turn left. At the time of writing, this would bring you into the former Russell furniture factory. The two illustrations show two sides of the venture in the 1920s when Gordon Russell was in charge of it: machine production inside the factory, and careful respect for Cotswold building traditions outside.

A mortising machine in the Russell workshops, c. 1928
(Courtesy of the Gordon Russell Trust)

The Russell workshops, including a barn used as showrooms
(Courtesy of the Gordon Russell Trust)

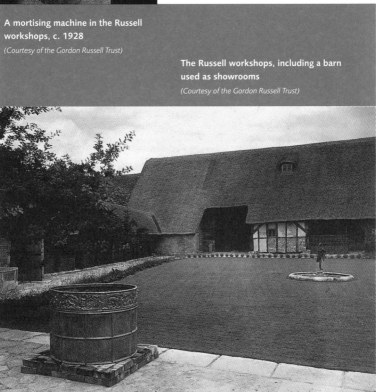

By the time you read this, the present buildings will almost certainly have been demolished and the site redeveloped, for the Russell works have moved to Worcester. But one may survive, as it has been listed:

A long, low building (5) of Cotswold stone with a red-tiled roof alongside Back Lane. It was designed, probably in the 1920s, by Leslie Mansfield, an architect popular with some progressive designers. (He also designed Gordon Russell's house, Kingcombe, above Chipping Campden.) His work here has a feeling of Arts and Crafts updated: the fat band of concrete running round the building, its face textured with Norfolk reed, was perhaps intended as a marriage of old and new, tradition and modernity.

As you pass this building you move from the backlands of the Russell furniture firm to the backlands of

The Lygon Arms (6). Facing you is a small stone building with two circular windows and a central chimney. This was built as the hotel laundry, probably in 1915, and designed by C. E. Bateman. On the same side of the road, behind the hotel, is Orchard Cottage, a very fancy square thatched job, designed by Bateman in about 1920 as staff accommodation. On the right is the inner courtyard of the hotel itself, lined with 20th-century extensions for the Russell family. At the far end on the right is a row of garages designed by Bateman in 1919, each bay flanked by columns. (The fortunes of the Lygon were made by motor tourism and Henry Ford was a guest.) This range was extended in 1926 by Leslie Mansfield, ending in a very romantic tower.

From here you can either return along Back Lane to the green, or you can continue for about 120 metres and then, before Back Lane narrows, turn right across the surgery car park and into the High Street.

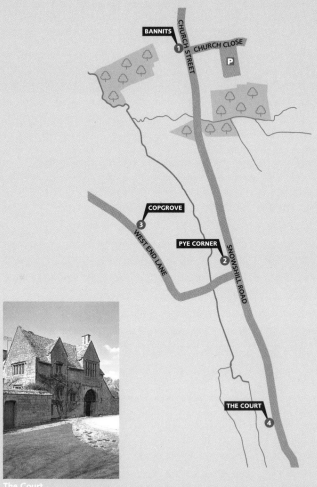

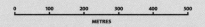
The Court

0   100   200   300   400   500
METRES

● The red dots mark the most important
  buildings on each walk. More are
  referred to in the text.

*From the War Memorial, go past the Broadway
Hotel and in front of you, as you turn into Church
Street, you can just see the gables of Abbot's Grange
over the big yew hedge. Abbot's Grange is one of the
most important buildings in Broadway. But the
house cannot be seen without intruding. A full
account of it is given on pp. 7–9.*

**Abbot's Grange, from the east,
c. 1900**
(Courtesy of the National Monuments Record)

In Church Street on the right, opposite the Crown and Trumpet, is

Bannits (1), a handsome 17th-century house set back behind a large walnut tree. In 1912-13 C. E. Bateman added the long wing to the north whose roughcast sides you can see down the lane. At the back, this wing encloses a delightful paved garden. The client was Mr Rees Price, a dentist from Glasgow who used to spend the summer at the Lygon Arms and retired to Broadway. He had a fine collection of 18th-century drinking glasses and sparked off S. B. Russell's interest in them.

The garden at the back of Bannits

Continue past St Michael and All Angels and as you pass Austin House you are almost out in the country. About 400 metres further on, after a row of houses set back on the right, you will come to a row of more picturesque houses, also on the right, at

Pye Corner (2). The first and smaller houses show how skilful C. E. Bateman could be when handling small Cotswold houses, whether he was repairing, enlarging, or building new. All the work was done for T. L. Parke of Pye Corner House. First, Meadowside, a stone cottage extended in 1936, with a cruck-framed thatched cottage next door at no. 39; then nos 41 and 43, a new house of 1936, or rather two houses but Bateman plays down the semi-detached look; then nos 45-7, a completely plain rebuilding job of 1937 but note the subtle variation in the width of the dormers; then no. 49, Pye Corner Stone Cottage, a rebuilding of 1924 with a handsome curved staircase projection to the road; then Pye Corner Cottage, extended southwards in 1930, but by Guy Pemberton, not Bateman.

After these small houses comes a big one, Pye Corner House, with a plain front to Snowshill Road. Turn right down West End Land and then look back to get a better look: the garden front shows more 17th- and 20th-century work.

Continue along West End Lane. On the right is **Pye Corner Farm**, *where the boarded range was added for T. L. Parke by Bateman in 1923. Carry on for about 100 metres and on the right is*

Copgrove (3). You can see early 20th-century parts from the entrance, but you will need the help of the illustrations for the garden front, which is screened by trees in summer.

For two or three hundred years a farmhouse stood alongside the road on the land where Copgrove now stands. In 1910 C. E. Bateman designed a scheme to fit the house for modern use, for G. A. Sewell, of Albert Hall Mansions, Kensington, in London. For the sake of privacy, the house was moved away from the road. For the sake of the view, the former road front became the garden front and, more drastically, the new garden front was reversed from left to right so that, for instance, the two-storey gabled bay stood to the left, not the right, of the door. For the sake of modern accommodation and comfort, the roof was raised several feet and a service wing was added.

Soon after the reconstruction of West End (as the house was then known), Sewell sold it to R. S. Peirse Duncombe of Broadway, and in 1911-12 Duncombe added a music room at the east end designed by Guy Pemberton.

West End (now Copgrove) before alteration

The same front reversed and rebuilt
(Courtesy of Country Life Picture Library)

Go back down West End Lane, noticing the garden fronts of the Pye Corner houses. At Pye Corner turn right, past the decent Cotswold-style bus stop of 1944. Then, on the right, **The Old Orchard**, *an effortlessly pretty, low house of 1932 by Bateman. Then, after about 300 metres, on the right just before St Eadburga's church, comes*

The Court (4). The part facing the road, with its handsome arched entrance, was probably originally the gatehouse or entrance to stables for nearby Broadway Court, demolished in 1773. Like much of the land between here and Broadway, it formed part of the Middle Hill estate, of which the big house is up on the hill, south-east of the church. From the mid-1870s the estate belonged to Edgar Flower, a member of the Stratford-on-Avon brewing family, who took old buildings seriously – he was a member of the Society for the Protection of Ancient Buildings. In 1898 he had the house altered and enlarged for his daughter Rita when she married Mr Ayshford Sanford. Guy Dawber was the architect and he added a drawing room, kitchen and bedrooms in a long range to the west, parallel with the entrance front.

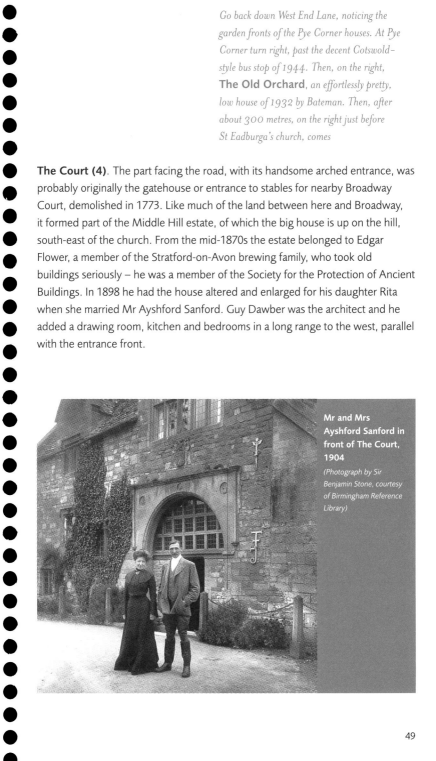

Mr and Mrs Ayshford Sanford in front of The Court, 1904
(Photograph by Sir Benjamin Stone, courtesy of Birmingham Reference Library)

If you walk towards the church and turn back, you will see the south front of the house, roughly as in the illustration. Dawber's additions, running back from the left-hand gable, simply extended the building in the manner of the original, so that one cannot see where the old stops and the new starts – except for one small but significant point. The client asked that the drawing-room window facing south should be glazed with plate glass instead of leaded lights for the sake of the view. The original builders would not have done that, for plate glass was not invented in the 17th century – nor would they have understood the modern notion of a 'view'.

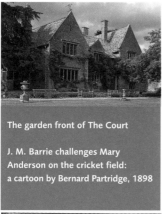

The garden front of The Court

J. M. Barrie challenges Mary Anderson on the cricket field: a cartoon by Bernard Partridge, 1898

On the other side of the road, past the church, are the entrance gates to Middle Hill. Past this is the cricket ground where Mary Anderson's XI used to play against a team of artists and writers led by the author of Peter Pan, *J. M. Barrie. Though this was an annual event, Mary Anderson never really understood the game, and always called it 'Crickets'.*

From here you can walk back along the road to Broadway or, after about 300 metres, you can take the footpath on the right opposite Mill Hay House. This will bring you back to the High Street just below the Leamington Road.

Chipping Campden

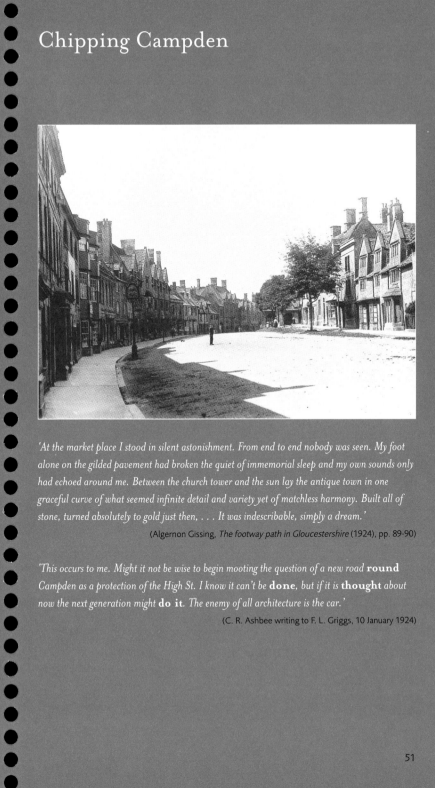

'At the market place I stood in silent astonishment. From end to end nobody was seen. My foot
alone on the gilded pavement had broken the quiet of immemorial sleep and my own sounds only
had echoed around me. Between the church tower and the sun lay the antique town in one
graceful curve of what seemed infinite detail and variety yet of matchless harmony. Built all of
stone, turned absolutely to gold just then, . . . It was indescribable, simply a dream.'

(Algernon Gissing, *The footway path in Gloucestershire* (1924), pp. 89-90)

'This occurs to me. Might it not be wise to begin mooting the question of a new road **round**
Campden as a protection of the High St. I know it can't be **done**, but if it is **thought** about
now the next generation might **do it**. The enemy of all architecture is the car.'

(C. R. Ashbee writing to F. L. Griggs, 10 January 1924)

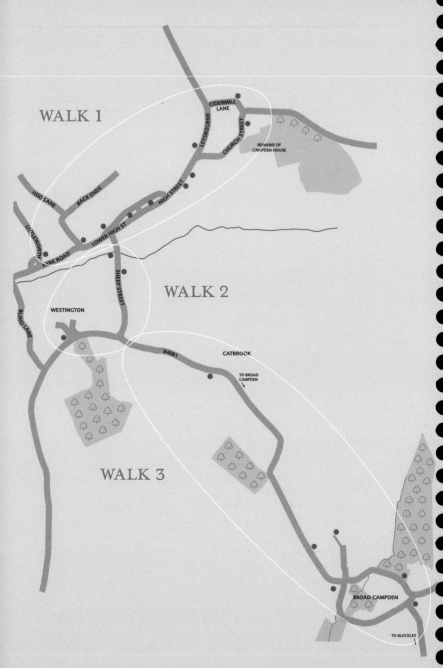

WALK 1

WALK 2

WALK 3

CIDERMILL LANE

LETSBOURNE

CHURCH STREET

REMAINS OF CAMPDEN HOUSE

HOO LANE

BACK ENDS

HIGH STREET

LITTLEWORTH

PARK ROAD

LOWER HIGH ST

SHEEP STREET

WESTINGTON

BLIND LANE

B4081

CATBROOK

TO BROAD CAMPDEN

BROAD CAMPDEN

TO BLOCKLEY

● *The red dots mark the most important buildings on each walk. More are referred to in the text.*

Planning your walks

Chipping Campden aims to control the number of its visitors more than Broadway does. As a result, there is no public car park. There are public loos in Sheep Street, near the junction with the High Street. To jugde distances, see the scale on the maps that accompany each walk.

Walk 1: Church Street, High Street, Lower High Street and Park Road, starts at the magnificent parish church of St James, goes all the way along the High Street and ends with the 1950s housing estate at Littleworth. It is a long, detailed walk and it will probably take longer than any other in this book. But I hope you will not be tempted to skip it, for the story of Arts and Crafts in Campden converges on the High Street, just as the life of Campden does. It is all here: F. L. Griggs at home; Fred Hart the passionate collector; the Guild of Handicraft's plays; printing at the Alcuin Press.

Walk 2: Sheep Street and Westington, is short but important, because it includes the Old Silk Mill which used to be the workshops of C. R. Ashbee's Guild of Handicraft. In the Old Silk Mill you can visit the workshop of Hart Silversmiths, which is in direct succession to the guild. The rest of the walk explores Westington, a hamlet on the edge of Campden with several large farmhouses, forming an interesting contrast to the close-packed architecture of the High Street.

Walk 3: Catbrook and Broad Campden, explores the little village of Broad Campden, about a mile and a half from Chipping Campden. The whole village is pretty, but its centrepiece is the Norman Chapel, a 12th-century chapel with later additions which was carefully and movingly transformed into a modern house by C. R. Ashbee in 1905-7. You can drive to Broad Campden in five minutes, but you can walk there in half an hour, and then you would have the pleasure of walking back to Chipping Campden across the fields.

The history of Chipping Campden

The best way to understand the history of Chipping Campden is to follow the first part of Walk 1, down the High Street. It starts at the parish church of St James, whose present form and architectural glory belong mainly to the late Middle Ages, when Chipping Campden was a national centre for the trade in wool, then England's principal export. Wool laid the foundations of Campden's prosperity.

From the church, we go past the Almshouses of 1612 which, like the Market Hall in the High Street, were given to the town by Sir Baptist Hicks, a wealthy London merchant and lord of the manor. By that time, the wool trade had passed from Campden, leaving it dependent on agriculture and the commercial life of a small country town. And we continue into the High Street where, vanishing into its curve, are house upon house of 16th-, 17th- and 18th-century date, almost all of Cotswold stone. There were shifts in Campden's economic fortunes during these times – silk-weaving was important for a time in the 18th century – but the houses themselves speak of a quiet, continuing prosperity.

And so into the 19th century. Throughout this century of change, Campden's population varied between about 1700 and 2000 people. In the High Street the town hall was rebuilt in the early 19th century, a new grammar school was built in 1863, and a new police station in 1871. These modern public buildings bear witness to Campden's town life.

In the early twentieth century artists and craftsmen began to settle in the town, led by the Arts and Crafts architect and designer C. R. Ashbee. These newcomers were apt to overlook the modern life of the town. For them the curving High Street, quiet in the summer sun, was a beautiful, jumbled, pre-industrial dream. They were, though they would hate the thought, the forerunners of the tourists who have flocked to Campden increasingly since the 1950s. And we are their successors.

Poppet's Alley, behind the High Street,
Chipping Campden, c. 1900
(Photograph by Jesse Taylor, courtesy of the
Guild of Handicraft Trust)

WALK 1: Church Street, High Street, Lower High Street and Park Road

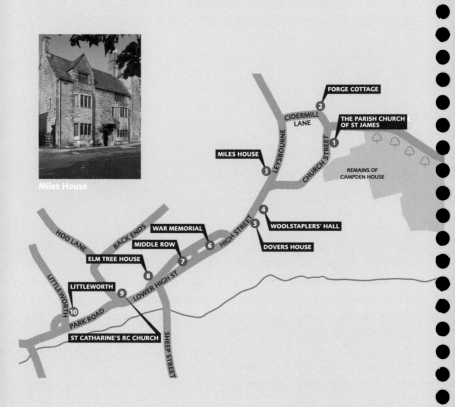

Miles House

FORGE COTTAGE

CIDERMILL LANE

THE PARISH CHURCH OF ST JAMES

MILES HOUSE

3

2

1

LEYSBOURNE

CHURCH STREET

REMAINS OF CAMPDEN HOUSE

HOO LANE

BACK ENDS

WAR MEMORIAL

MIDDLE ROW

ELM TREE HOUSE

4

5

WOOLSTAPLERS' HALL

HIGH STREET

6

DOVERS HOUSE

7

8

LITTLEWORTH

9

LOWER HIGH ST

10

PARK ROAD

LITTLEWORTH

ST CATHARINE'S RC CHURCH

SHEEP STREET

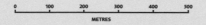

| 0 | 100 | 200 | 300 | 400 | 500 |

METRES

• *The red dots mark the most important buildings on each walk. More are referred to in the text.*

The Parish church of St James (1). The glory of the
church consists partly in the elegance and richness of its
late-medieval architecture, and partly in the 17th-century
tombs of the Hicks family in the south chapel.

The west window was designed by H. Ellis Wooldridge and
made by James Powell & Sons, 1876-7, before Arts and
Crafts attitudes to stained glass had developed.

The east window was designed and made by Henry Payne
in 1924-5, incorporating fragments of 15th-century stained
glass in the tracery. Payne was one of a talented group of
Arts and Crafts designers in Birmingham. He moved to
Amberley in the Cotswolds in 1909, and worked there until
his death in 1939. Payne had a talent for treating a window
as a single, dramatic composition but here, because it is a
large window with five openings, he filled it with static
figures. The small Biblical scenes at the bottom of each
opening show how vivid his compositions could be.

A Biblical scene from
the east window,
by Henry Payne,
1924-5

The differences between the west and east windows reveal important themes in
Arts and Crafts stained glass. The west window was *designed* by Wooldridge and
made by a firm of glassmakers, and its glass is pure and translucent. But Arts and
Crafts stained-glass artists liked designer and maker to be one, and they liked to
emphasise the texture of the material. So Payne was both designer and maker in
1924-5, and he used dense glass in glowing colours.

The communion rails in the chancel and the screens to either side were designed
by Norman Jewson in the late 1940s. Jewson was based in the south Cotswolds,
near Cirencester, but he built a good deal in Campden. The north chapel was
refurnished in about 1950 to designs by Jewson, executed by J. W. Pyment & Co.
In 1968 panels of local scenes, originally made for the east window, were inserted
in the east window by Henry Payne's son, Edward.

Of work by Ashbee and his Guild of Handicraft, there is only one small Boer War
memorial plaque just south of the chancel arch. This is because Ashbee and the
then vicar of Campden, Thomas Carrington, did not get on.

Several Arts and Crafts people are buried in **the churchyard** *and the standard of 20th-century lettering on gravestones is high. So it is worth turning left out of the church porch and walking down the corridor of yews, to the lower graveyard*

Follow the grass path until you get to the large yew tree on your right. Turn left and walk towards the gate into Station Road. The second last gravestone on your right is for Jim Pyment, cabinetmaker of the Guild of Handicraft and later a builder. Facing the stone, look ahead to the other side of the grass path, and slightly to your right you will see a cluster of gravestones. A small plain stone in the middle is for Arthur and Georgie Gaskin, jewellers and illustrators.

Take the grass path back to the yew tree, turn right and start to walk towards the slope you first came down. In the third row on the left, about ten stones along, is the stone for Bernard Sleigh, with an artist's palette and three brushes. Then look up towards the church: almost directly ahead and slightly to the right, in a row close to the wall is the gravestone of Benjamin Chandler, an American patron of Arts and Crafts work, beautifully lettered.

Now go to the end of this row leaving Chandler's stone behind you. When you come to the grass path with birdbath on your right, turn left and walk straight towards the east perimeter wall. You will be looking towards open ground. One of the stones with its inscription facing the wall is for Gordon Russell's father, Sydney Bolton Russell, carved by Gordon Russell.

Gordon Russell carving his father's gravestone
(Photograph by Sam Lambert)

Now turn round and walk back up the path towards the steps leading to the upper graveyard. As you go, notice on your left stones for Henry Hart, gold- and silversmith, George Hart, guildsman and silversmith, and Gordon Russell himself, an eccentric stone carved by John Skelton with a quotation from D. H. L[awrence?] round the edge. Carry on towards the steps and to your left is Oliver John Russell, one of Gordon Russsell's sons. From this point you get good views of the surviving pavilions and ruins of Campden House, which was built in 1613-20 by Sir Baptist Hicks. If it stood today it would be one of the great Jacobean houses of England. It was destroyed in 1645.

Leave the churchyard by the Church Street entrance.
Facing you is **The Tithe House**, *designed in*
1940 by Norman Jewson for Christopher Whitfield
who came to Campden in the early 1920s as a
young poet, and later wrote a history of the town.
The house was enlarged in 1975. Immediately
on your left are the lodges and gateway to
Campden House.

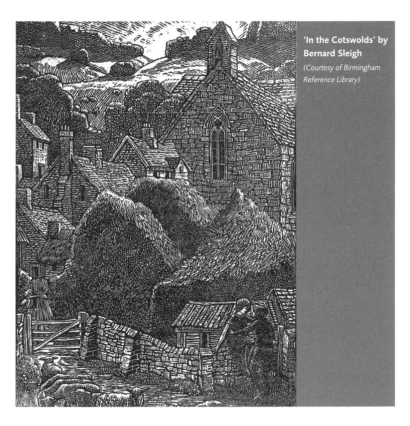

'In the Cotswolds' by
Bernard Sleigh
(Courtesy of Birmingham
Reference Library)

At this point you can turn right down Church Street
to the junction with Station Road and Cidermill
Lane. On the right past Station Road is

Forge Cottage (2). Bernard Sleigh, mural painter, stained-glass artist, illustrator
and wood engraver, lived here from his retirement from teaching in Birmingham

in the mid-1930s until his death in 1954. In his twenties Sleigh had an illness of the brain and for the rest of his life suffered from sudden and powerful visions. Round 1900 the imagery of the Arts and Crafts movement, itself visionary, served him well enough, and his Cotswold fantasy illustrated here is easy and romantic. But his work could also be savage (cartoon-like visions of the horrors of capitalism), bizarre (fully-populated fairylands) and hallucinogenic (he experimented with mescal, guided by the sexologist Havelock Ellis). All this in a cosy Cotswold cottage.

Now go back along Church Street. On the right, after the church, are the **Almshouses** *of 1612, built by Sir Baptist Hicks and perhaps the finest early 17th-century building in the Cotswolds. At the bottom of Church Street, turn briefly right into Leysbourne and, almost opposite the cast-iron pump, with two two-storey bays, is*

Miles House (3). In the early 19th century, two 17th-century cottages on this site were recast as one house; in 1917 this was further altered and refronted for the elderly Miss Helen Macaulay to the designs of F. L. Griggs, artist and etcher. The front is a perfect example of Arts and Crafts infill, sensitive to the High Street (plainer than its older neighbours, leaving the show to them); sensitive to materials (the baldness of the bays emphasises their 'stoniness'); and just a little quirky (see the odd junction of the porch and right-hand bay.) Janet Ashbee, who perhaps regretted her husband had not designed it, referred unkindly to 'great stone mullioned orioles to rooms you can't swing a mouse in'.

Now turn back towards the High Street, which bends south-westwards from here. This makes it awkward to refer to the points of the compass. For the rest of this walk you are facing down the High Street, away from the parish church, and buildings are simply described as 'on the right' or 'on the left'.

On the left, just after the ornate Bedfont House of 1740, are

Woolstaplers' Hall and Woolstaplers' House (4). Woolstaplers' Hall is late 14th-century in origin and connected with the medieval wool merchant Robert

Calf; Woolstaplers' House is of various later dates. C. R. and Janet Ashbee lived in both from 1902, when they arrived with the Guild of Handicraft, to 1911. In 1902 the house had a suburban-sounding name like 'The Laurels' and there was a 19th-century bay window on the ground floor, under the 14th-century oriel. Over the years, the Ashbees moved the house back, so to speak, into the 'good history' of the Middle Ages. First they changed the name to Woolstaplers' Hall, placing it confidently in the centre of the medieval wool trade. Then in 1903 they cleared out partitions from the upper room behind the oriel, exposing a 15th-century timber roof and a Tudor fireplace. This room became the intellectual heart of the house, a place for big discussions, reading and writing, folk songs with the guildsmen in the evenings. And they made their own mark on the building, inserting a stained-glass window in the tip of the gable at the back, with a design by Paul Woodroffe of ASH and BEE. Later, in 1909, they explored the house further, planning to expose timber-framing in one wing, but in the end they simply removed the 19th-century bay window and put an entrance in its place.

Stained-glass window by Paul Woodroffe in the upper room of Woolstaplers' Hall

On the same side as Woolstaplers' Hall, opposite the Seymour House Hotel, is the early 18th-century **Braithwaite House,** *with urns on its parapet. This was used by the Guild of Handicraft as a hostel for unmarried craftsmen. When the Ashbees had visitors they often stayed there, and in 1902 the architect Cecil Brewer, not appreciating the egalitarian spirit of the guild, left his boots outside his door one night. The guildsmen simply put a brush and a box of blacking in them.*

Then, on the right, opposite the Lygon Arms, is **Westcote House**, *early 18th-century but very much in the Cotswold vernacular. It was repaired in 1926 by Norman Jewson and F. L. Griggs. From about that date the house was occupied by the Kingsley Weavers, run by Leo and Eileen Baker. Eileen Baker had learned to weave in Ditchling, Sussex, with the pioneer of modern hand-loom weaving in England, Ethel Mairet. The Bakers employed local women and the actual looms were in a converted barn on the other side of the High Street, behind Dovers House.*

Then, on the left, three properties beyond the Lygon Arms, is

Dovers House (5), a beautiful early Georgian house in which F. L. Griggs lived from 1906 to 1930. He was a lonely bachelor for many years, and would ask friends in Campden to stay, or just to sit with him while he worked. The house was unkempt and Griggs wrote that he lived very simply, – 'from necessity – not out of any beggarly Simple Life humbug!' But with time simplicity came to include 18th-century furniture and silver. Then, around the end of the First World War, he experienced an aesthetic conversion from Georgian to Arts and Crafts and Alec Miller wrote to Ashbee: 'How curious is his "volte face" – he has got rid of all his 18th century furniture & table silver & so on – & has his house all furnished with modern furniture of Gimson's in raw oak – & Iron candlesticks replace the Sheffield plate ones - & he wants to destroy all machinery & be a real "modern mediaevalist" like Eric Gill & Pepler. What a thing is man!' Inside the house, on the staircase, is a stained-glass panel of 'Little Miss Muffet' by Paul Woodroffe, dating from the late 1920s.

A little further on, on the right, in the handsome front of 1717 with a shallow bay to the ground floor, is **Trinder House.** *Fred Hart, a retired naval commander and brother of guildsmen Will and George Hart, lived here from 1924. Like his friend Charles Wade of Snowshill Manor, Fred Hart was a passionate, magpie-like collector. He and Wade hunted together, trading their finds. He kept the top half of the door to Trinder House open in most weathers, and could be seen sitting in his Aladdin's cave, surrounded by wooden bygones, T'ang Dynasty* figures, Viking and Persian shields, barometers, farm implements, ships' figureheads, 17th-century French firebacks, …The sale of Fred Hart's collection, when he died in 1971, took four days. Trinder House still belongs to the Hart family.

Still on the right, between the pavement and the road, is the heraldic **town sign**, designed by Wentworth Huyshe and his son Reynell in 1924 and erected at the millennium. Huyshe, a racy ex-journalist with a taste for heraldry and the Middle Ages, was the stepfather of Will, George and Fred Hart and settled in Campden in 1906.

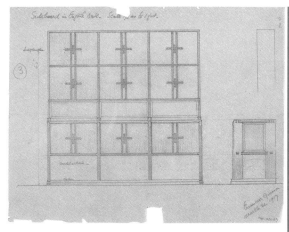

Drawing of a sideboard designed by Ernest Gimson for F. L. Griggs, 1917
(Courtesy of Cheltenham Art Gallery and Museum)

Then, next to the road on the right, comes the arcaded **Market Hall,** built by Sir Baptist Hicks in 1627, and a point of focus in the High Street. In 1942 it was offered for sale and eventually acquired by the conservationists of the Campden Trust, who presented it to the National Trust.

Go into the Market Hall and look back over the road from its arcades to the **Old King's Arms.** *This 16th-century building was one of the properties bought by the Campden Trust with a view to repairing it and selling it on. The work was done under the care of Norman Jewson and F. L. Griggs in 1929, exposing the timber framing of the upper storey. Leaving the Market Hall you come to the*

War Memorial (6). This is not just a cross but a complete scheme of a wall, a grassy plot linking the Market Hall and the Town Hall, and steps up from the lower road to the level of the cross. It was designed by F. L. Griggs in 1919 and carved by Alec Miller, as a memorial to the sixty Campden men who died in the First World War, and was the subject of fierce controversy in the town.

Next to the War Memorial is a bench on which you can sit and study the changes which Griggs and Jewson made in 1926 to the early 18th-century **Elsley House:** *they replaced the plate-glass shop windows with something more 18th-century-looking, and at the top got rid of a parapet and mansard roof.*

Elsley House before restoration
(Photograph by Jesse Taylor, courtesy of the Guild of Handicraft Trust)

Then comes the **Town Hall**, *medieval in origin but much altered at the beginning and end of the 19th century. This is where the Guild of Handicraft put on its plays every New Year. In 1903 they acted Ben Jonson's* The New Inn, *and the Earl of Gainsborough slept through much of a matinee* *performance, waking with a start when Prudence the Chambermaid stamped her foot in Act IV and cried 'Be damned for ignorance!'*

Leave the Town Hall on your left and you come into The Square, an open space which dilutes the experience of the High Street for a moment. It was used for sheep and cattle markets until the 1950s, and is still used for maypole dancing. Facing the Town Hall across The Square is

Middle Row (7). Like the Market Hall and Town Hall, this forms an island between the upper and lower roads. First there is a building with a gable like the Town Hall's, facing the Square. Go past this on the right and you will see a paved gap and a public path between this building and the next group, which consists of Island House, and Rosary Cottage facing in the opposite direction. When the Guild of Handicraft was at its height, it used Island House as a club, complete with a billiard room, bar and brand-new gramophone. This was very popular with the townspeople. In 1905-6 Ashbee carried out some very conservative repairs to Island House. From 1902 this western group of Middle Row also housed the bookbinding workshop under the direction of Annie Power, the first woman to be employed by the guild.

A brooch by Arthur and Georgie Gaskin, c. 1914
(Courtesy of Tadema Gallery)

Leaving Middle Row on your left, you come into another open space, at the junction with Sheep Street. On the left, shortly before Sheep Street, is **Camperdene House**, *where Arthur and Georgie Gaskin lived from 1924. They were perhaps the leading book illustrators and jewellers of the Arts and Crafts movement in Birmingham and, like many of their colleagues, retired to the Cotswolds, though they both went on working in Campden. Arthur died in 1928, and Georgie moved to Kent shortly afterwards, dying in 1934.*

Physical fitness class at the
Campden School of Arts and Crafts,
c. 1906
(Courtesy of the Ashbee family)

*On the right, facing the junction with Sheep
Street, is*

Elm Tree House (8), with three dormers and a pretty semi-circular wooden
window. There are several layers of Arts and Crafts history here. For some years
from 1902 Ashbee had his architectural office in this fine mid-17th-century house,
with a complete set of the writings of John Ruskin on the shelves.

In 1904 he set up the Campden School of Arts and Crafts here. Using the house
itself and a disused malt house at the back, he provided a library and classrooms
for cookery, woodwork, metalwork and enamelling. The upper floor of the malt
house was used as a gallery and lecture room, and there were classes outdoors
for gardening and physical fitness. The photograph of the physical fitness class
shows part of the malt house and other school buildings in the background.
Properties in Campden High Street are typically long, narrow, medieval plots with
many such buildings tucked in behind the street frontages.

The School closed down in 1916 and after that the malt house was used for
various craft purposes, including the Arts and Crafts exhibitions organised by the

Campden Society in the 1920s and 1930s. In early 1928 the young H. P. R. Finberg, son of the biographer of J. M. W. Turner, installed the machinery of his Alcuin Press in the malt house. His was not a 'private press', like Ashbee's Essex House Press or William Morris's Kelmscott Press. He used up-to-date machinery and operated commercially, mainly printing books for London publishers. But he had the same eye for quality as Arts and Crafts printers. In 1935 he moved the press to Welwyn Garden City.

Then, on the left, on the corner of Sheep Street, a gabled house with all the breadth and simplicity that Arts and Crafts architects admired, repaired by Norman Jewson in about 1930 and now the **Robert Welch Studio Shop**.

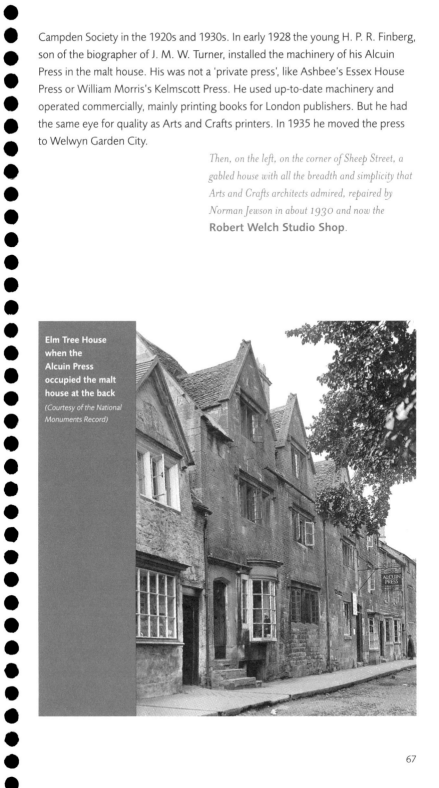

Elm Tree House when the Alcuin Press occupied the malt house at the back
(Courtesy of the National Monuments Record)

You are now in the Lower High Street. Continue for about 100 metres and on your left will be **Izod's Cottage**, which looks as if it is an old building much repaired, but is actually a new building by Ashbee of 1902 (not 1906 as it says beside the door), for W. N. Izod, of an old Campden farming family. Two cottages on the site were demolished and some of the materials used in this straightforward piece of Cotswold-style work.

The two cottages that became Izod's Cottage
(Photograph by Jesse Taylor, courtesy of the Guild of Handicraft Trust)

Almost opposite Izod's Cottage, on the corner of Lower High Street and Hoo Lane, is

St Catharine's Roman Catholic church (9). The church was built in 1891 in a festive late Gothic style which suits the town outstandingly well. The architect was W. Lunn of Malvern. Two of the leading local artist-craftsmen, F. L. Griggs and Paul Woodroffe, were Catholics and their work is represented in the church. Griggs designed the crucifix in the chancel arch (carved by Alec Miller), the pulpit and organ case. Woodroffe designed the Noel family window of 1909 in the south transept, the Macaulay and Lynch Staunton windows in the north aisle, the Lynch Staunton window in the south aisle and St Thomas More at the west end of the south aisle. In the churchyard, a cross designed by Griggs, and the **Priest's House** to the north, 1935 by Griggs and Guy Pemberton.

At this point you could make a short detour to the **Catholic cemetery**, *up Hoo Lane on the right, after the turning to Back Ends. Here the cross in the centre was designed by F. L. Griggs, who is buried with some of his family nearby.*

From the junction of Hoo Lane and Lower High Street, continue down Park Road which is lined more with cottages than houses. After about fifty metres, on the left, is **Pavement Cottage**, *an experiment of c. 1903. Ashbee could not be architect, but he gave a local builder general instructions, leaving him to sort out the plan and details. He thought the result very creditable. Could the Cotswold vernacular live without the help of London architects?*

Next but one on the same side, **Brooklyn**, *another case of two cottages turned into one, by Ashbee in 1903. The work was paid for by Rob Martin-Holland, a banker and one of the directors of the Guild of Handicraft Limited, who was thus giving Ashbee work and providing accommodation for guildsmen.*

**Houses on the Littleworth estate
just after completion**
*(Photograph by Roland Dyer, courtesy of the
Guild of Handicraft Trust)*

Littleworth (10). Here there is a prize-winning estate of houses designed by Pemberton and Bateman for the North Cotswold District Council in the 1950s. Guy Pemberton and T. R. Bateman were the two local architects most responsible for carrying the Arts and Crafts building tradition into the mid-20th century in the North Cotswolds. Note the Festival of Britain emblem carved on a gable-end facing towards Park Road. The earliest (and arguably the best) houses are the blocks of two and four with stone dressings on the west side of Littleworth. Though almost all are spoiled by intrusive new windows, they show how well suited the Arts and Crafts Cotswold style was to housing.

This walk started with a fine medieval parish church and ends with a 1950s council estate. Normally such a transition would involve a loss in architectural quality but here, surely, there has been gain. The walk has shown how well Arts and Crafts architects in the 20th century learned from the rich and versatile language of the Cotswold vernacular.

WALK 2: Sheep Street and Westington

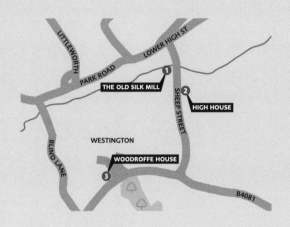

Westington

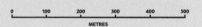

0   100   200   300   400   500
METRES

• The red dots mark the most important
buildings on each walk. More are
referred to in the text.

*We start from the junction of Sheep Street and the High Street, walking away from the High Street. Immediately on the right is a row of plain two-storey cottages, **Gordon Cottages**, built in 1901. When the Guild of Handicraft arrived in 1902 needing houses, they took a lease on these six. It was not a success. Herbert Osborn and his family took no. 6 and found a hearth too small to cook on and no garden. There was just a narrow yard at the back, with six outside lavatories in the middle. They had left a flat in Bethnal Green with privacy and internal plumbing. Mrs Osborn sat down and wept.*

After Gordon Cottages there is a sign saying 'The Guild' and a passage on the right, next to the tiny River Cam. The building at the end of the passage is

The Old Silk Mill (1). This is the building to which C. R. Ashbee brought the workshops of his Guild of Handicraft in 1902, from Mile End in East London. The building is still used for craft purposes, and one of the workshops, Hart Silversmiths, is in a direct line of descent from the silversmiths of the Guild. Hart Silversmiths always welcome visitors, and you may like to start by going into the building, and up the stairs on the right to their workshop. David Hart, who runs the workshop at the time of writing, is the grandson of one of the guild silversmiths, and you will find that his workshop looks little different from how it did in 1906, when the photograph illustrated here was taken.

The guild silversmiths' shop, c. 1906
(Photograph by Jesse Taylor, courtesy of the Guild of Handicraft Trust)

When you leave the building, cross over Sheep Street and look back. Refer also to the 1906 view of the other side of the building.

The mill was built about 1790 and produced silk for the ribbon trade in Coventry, but it is also the core building of the Arts and Crafts movement in Campden, and arguably the best surviving workshop site of the Arts and Crafts movement in Britain. Of other workshops comparable to Ashbee's, either the fabric has been destroyed, or craft activity has ceased; usually both. At the Old Silk Mill, both survive.

When the guildsmen arrived in the summer of 1902, a 12-horsepower oil engine was set up in a brick shed in the yard, to provide electric light for the workshops in winter. The blacksmiths went in outbuildings, and the other workshops filled the mill as follows: printers and offices on the ground floor; metalworkers and enamellers on the first; and cabinetmakers and woodcarvers on the second. Ashbee's office was in the house to the right of the mill in the photograph.

The memoirs of guildsmen do not say much about life in the workshops, so we have to make do with those of visitors. In 1906 the Swiss architect Hans Eduard von Berlepsch-Valendas came and thought the whole thing perfect: he saw happy workmen, views of beautiful gardens through the windows, hazy blue light on distant hills. 'Surely,' he wrote, 'it rains here sometimes ...'

The silk mill in about 1906

(Photograph by Jesse Taylor, courtesy of the Guild of Handicraft Trust)

After the Guild of Handicraft Limited went into liquidation in 1908, Jim Pyment, who had been foreman of the cabinetmakers, started a building and cabinetmaking business in the mill. In 1917 he bought the building, and it is still in the possession of the Pyment family. Other former guildsmen working in the building became his tenants, and of these, the silversmith George Hart carried on longest on the first floor, handing his workshop on to his son Henry and grandson David. In 1955 Robert Welch, a silversmith and cutlery designer fresh from the Royal College of Art, began to rent part of the top floor. He worked in the building for the rest of his life, building up an international reputation as a silversmith and designer. At first he knew nothing about Ashbee or the guild, but slowly the building gave up its story, as he stumbled across relics of the guild in his workshop and listened to old men's tales.

At the time of writing, things are changing in the Old Silk Mill. The Pyment building firm has moved its main office elsewhere, though it keeps a presence in the building. Following Robert Welch's death in 2000, his firm is run by his children, and his younger son William, also trained at the Royal College of Art, is taking over as designer. On the first floor, the Hart workshop carries on, almost as unchanging as the building itself.

From the Old Silk Mill, carry on down Sheep Street, past the garage, and immediately on the left is

High House (2), built for Lord Gainsborough to Ashbee's design and lived in at first by Archie Ramage, a guild printer. It was called High House because Ashbee piled his design on top of the walls of a ruined cottage. Some Arts and Crafts architects leaned towards austerity in the Cotswolds, and in this spirit Ashbee left off the mouldings round windows and doors that usually enrich Cotswold buildings, though he did use local masonry techniques – the stone roof-tiles are graded in size.

As you carry on to the end of Sheep Street you enter Westington, an outlier of Campden where some of the larger farmhouses were built. As the road bears round to the right, notice **Pike Cottage** *with its luxuriant thatch on the left. From 1906–1934, when it was known as Pike House, it was the home of Wentworth Huyshe. Follow the road round, and second on the left is* **Porchester Cottage**, *a neat and substantial building of about 1935, designed by Norman Jewson for the guild woodcarver, Will Hart. Continuing on the right side of the road, you come to a wrought-iron gate between circular columns where you can see* **Shepherd's Close**, *which looks like a small manor house, but is in fact four cottages converted into one in the 1930s. Then, on the same side, the 17th-century* **Old Manor House** *by the roadside, and the 18th-century* **Wool Barn**, *set back, were both restored in 1940 by T. R. Bateman.* **Westington House**, *attached to the Manor House, was restored in 1866 by George Hunt of Evesham, and is a good example of a 17th-century house Victorianised, before sensitivity to the Cotswold vernacular had arrived. Facing Westington House across the green is*

Woodroffe House (3), repaired and enlarged by Ashbee in 1904 for the stained-glass artist Paul Woodroffe. The old photograph shows the original building in the distance. Ashbee's description of the repairs shows the brisk but conservative spirit in which he worked: 'When I came to handle it, the box & yew had grown out of all reason, the thatch was open, the stones covered with moss, and the damp thick upon them. We gutted the interior, re-lit the rooms, opened out the great ingle in the houseplace, turned the stone bread oven to service as a cupboard, re-glazed the windows, re-thatched the roof, and damp coursed the whole house.'

His principal addition was the shallow gabled wing to the front. It was not large spatially, but it transformed the house as seen from the green.

Across the road from Woodroffe House are Rose Cottages. Arthur Cameron, guild metalworker, lived in no. 2. The photograph shows him with his wife, brother and child. The Ashbees pasted this into their journal and Janet Ashbee wrote underneath it 'Picture of reformed Cockneys in Arcadia'.

**The Cameron family in front of
2 Rose Cottages**
(Courtesy of the Cameron family)

From here you can walk back the way you came, or down Blind Lane. Or, if you face Woodroffe House and then turn right, you can walk back across the fields to Park Road.

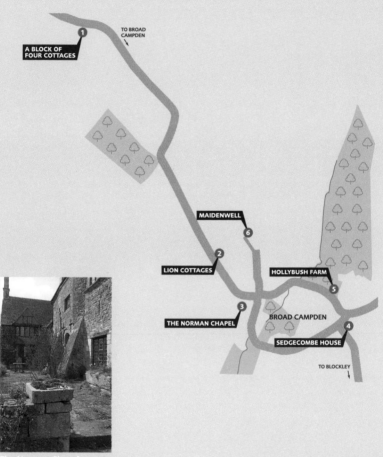

A BLOCK OF
FOUR COTTAGES

1

TO BROAD
CAMPDEN

MAIDENWELL

6

LION COTTAGES

2

HOLLYBUSH FARM

5

THE NORMAN CHAPEL

3

BROAD CAMPDEN

SEDGECOMBE HOUSE

4

TO BLOCKLEY

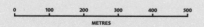

The Norman Chapel

0   100   200   300   400   500

METRES

• The red dots mark the most important
buildings on each walk. More are
referred to in the text.

Broad Campden is about one and a half miles south-east of Chipping Campden. To get there go down Sheep Street, turn left at the end of Sheep Street on the B4081, and the road will take you there. If you have the time to walk it, do so. It is much pleasanter, and you can walk back from Broad Campden across the fields.

After about half a mile, there is Catbrook Gardens on the left, just before the road turns to the right. Opposite Catbrook Gardens on the right is

a block of **four cottages (1)**, designed by Ashbee and built in 1905-6. The illustration shows them as built, with the roofs thatched. Ashbee built the houses not of local stone but of brick covered with roughcast, perhaps for reasons of cost. He thought he could create a good effect simply by good proportions, and felt roughcast was a quiet material that would fit in anywhere. But the design of such simple roughcast houses is vulnerable to even small changes, and the changes in these houses have been large. Round the corner, on the same side of the road, are **Maryvale** and **Catbrook Furlong,** a semi-detached pair by Ashbee of 1902-3, also of roughcast brick. Here again there have been changes and the houses have lost their original Cotswold-stone tiles.

Thatched cottages designed by Ashbee
(Photograph by Jesse Taylor, courtesy of the Guild of Handicraft Trust)

Plan of Lion Cottages

The garden front of the Norman Chapel

Continue along the road, and as you come into Broad Campden, after the telephone box on the left, are **Lion Cottages (2)**. *Ashbee altered and repaired a block of four dilapidated early 19th – century cottages in 1902 to form these two. As the bedroom plans show, they were still very small.*

If you are in a car, it is best after Lion Cottages to follow the road round to the left and then park in front of St Michael's church.

Standing with your back to St Michael's church, you can see part of

The Norman Chapel (3), standing up above the hedge. The house has a long history and a complicated plan, and is partly hidden from view, so patience is needed to understand it. A church was built here in the early twelfth century, and as you stand with your back to St Michael's you are looking at the nave of that church from the east (the chancel has been destroyed). Beyond you can see roughcast additions by C. R. Ashbee. In the illustration, the Norman part is on the right. In about 1400 an upper floor was inserted above the nave as you can see, and a priest's house was built at the west end. You can see the gable end of the priest's house in the illustration, to the left of the Norman building. For several hundred years the building was used as a farmhouse.

When Ashbee first saw it in 1903 the nave of the church and the priest's house were in a ruinous state. In 1905-7 he repaired and enlarged this building as a house for Ethel Coomaraswamy, sister of the guild jeweller Fred Partridge, and her husband Ananda, a tall, dark-eyed Anglo-Sinhalese. Ashbee rebuilt and buttressed the nave walls and gave the spaces in the old building big, simple uses, music room, library, dining room. His additions were confined to a two-storey bay overlooking the terrace and a service wing at the north-east corner. Both these additions were built of roughcast brick, to mark them off from the old work. Ashbee was a lifelong member of the Society for the Protection of Ancient Buildings, and here he was following the Society's principle that new work added to an old building should be 'simple and unpretentious, of good material and workmanship, and frankly the production of the present day'.

Ashbee would have liked to live in the house himself, but he could not have asked for better clients than the Coomaraswamys. They furnished the house with the work of the guild, and hung it with textiles from India and Morris & Co. Janet Ashbee wrote 'Both of them live in their enchanted chapel which glows rose-colour with linen and Morris hangings and oriental crimsons – like two does, creatures that you cannot gossip with, and that yet have something more human about them than the most ordinary of us.'

The Coomaraswamys moved out in 1911 and the Ashbees, whose first child had just been born, were able to rent it from them. Three more daughters were born there. Ashbee was away for much of the First World War, and the Norman Chapel, which was so romantic in peacetime, became a domestic fortress for his wife Janet, sometimes idyllic but sometimes full of too many things – loneliness, childbirth, burst pipes, absconding ponies. They left Broad Campden in 1919 and the house was sold to Arthur Brampton, a bicycle manufacturer from Birmingham. Later it belonged to a sculptress, Mabel Deakin, who enlarged it to the south and west of Ashbee's service wing.

The barn that became Sedgecombe House
(Photograph courtesy of Allan Warmington)

Go down the road, leaving the Norman Chapel on your right, but keep looking back to catch glimpses of it. The best view comes after the turn in the road as you are climbing up; but in summer even that will be screened by trees. To get a full and open view of the whole house, it is necessary to go up the Blockley road for about half a mile.

Carry on until you come to the T–junction with the road to Blockley. On the corner is

Sedgecombe House (4) which was converted from a barn to a second home in 1926 by W. W. Blair-Fish, who wrote for *Punch* and the *Sunday Times* and acted very successfully as his own architect. The builder was Joe Warmington, a Campden man. The illustrations show the transformation, which must have been a common sight in the North Cotswolds at this time.

Leaving Sedgecombe House on your right, you will come to a lane marked 'Unsuitable for motors'. About fifty metres down this lane, on the right, is

Hollybush Farm (5). After the Guild of Handicraft Limited went into liquidation in 1908, Ashbee bought this 70-acre farm so that the craftsmen who stayed in Campden might work on allotments and smallholdings there, and have a second string to their bow. The money to buy it came from Joseph Fels, a millionaire philanthropist from Philadelphia who believed in settling people on the land. It was a success, but was cut short by the First World War.

Sedgecombe House that used to be a barn
(Photograph courtesy of Allan Warmington)

Continue up the lane and it will bring you back to St Michael's church. From here you could make a little exploration: follow the left-hand lane above the church until you come to the end of the road by the Friends Meeting House. Opposite this is a gap in the wall and a narrow path. This will bring you to the drive in front of

Maidenwell (6), a 17th-century house enlarged and remodelled by F. L. Griggs in 1914 for a member of the Earl of Gainsborough's family. You are on a public right of way, and should keep to it to avoid trespassing. To the right is a former barn, now Maidenwell Cottage, and the house itself can be glimpsed through the cartway. From here you must go back the way you came, unless you are on foot, in which case you could stay on the footpath and walk back across the fields to Chipping Campden.

The villages round about

Arts and Crafts work in the north Cotswolds was by no means confined to Broadway and Chipping Campden. Here are short notes on what you can see in the villages round about:

Aston-sub-Edge The Village Club and Hiatts Farm, both of 1905, are by Guy Dawber, who probably also designed the War Memorial.

Blockley This might have been a great site of Arts and Crafts pilgrimage, for William Morris and the potter William De Morgan visited Blockley in 1880, thinking of moving their workshops there. But they decided against it. De Morgan later said he thought it was a Minton's Paradise Lost.

Bourton-on-the-Hill In the parish church, the pulpit is by Guy Dawber, 1889, the surround to the main altar by C. E. Bateman, 1925, and a reredos in the north aisle also by Bateman, 1935, with panels painted by Sydney Meteyard, a Birmingham Arts and Crafts artist. Porch House, in the main street, was converted by Bateman for himself in 1924.

Buckland The 1921 reredos in the parish church was designed by Alexander Fisher. Buckland Manor, near the church, was enlarged to the south-west in 1910-13 by Andrew Prentice.

Ebrington In the parish church, the memorial tablet to the Rev. C. E. Hornby is by Eric Gill. Guy Dawber did additions to the rear of Ebrington Manor in 1899, and later, around 1925.

Hidcote In the famous gardens at Hidcote Manor, created by Lawrence Johnston between 1907 and 1930, the earliest part, immediately south-west of the house, shows strong Arts and Crafts influence. The north-west wing of Hidcote Manor itself, of c. 1910, is probably by Norman Jewson, who also altered and restored Hidcote House in 1924-5.

Moreton-in-Marsh On the outskirts of the town, Wells Folly is a small country house designed by Guy Dawber in 1904-5.

Saintbury C. R. Ashbee did not get on with the vicar of Chipping Campden, but he did with the vicar of Saintbury, so the Ashbee family worshipped here. Ashbee repaired the church in 1906-7 and designed the bosses on the chancel roof and the chandelier in the chancel. Alec Miller, formerly of the Guild of Handicraft, carved the reredos in the north transept, 1925, the figure of St Nicholas on the north door, 1911, and the war memorial, 1920. The screen to the north transept is by Ernest Gimson, c. 1902.

Snowshill Tower Close, at the top of the hill, is of c. 1916 by C. E. Bateman for Sydney Bolton Russell, with panelling throughout by Gordon Russell. Snowshill Manor was bought in 1919 by the eccentric Arts and Crafts architect and collector Charles Wade, who carried out a thorough restoration and filled the house with his bizarre collection, which is still there. The Japanese suits of armour linger in the mind. The Arts and Crafts architect M. H. Baillie Scott provided plans for the garden in 1920.

Stanton In 1906 a Lancashire architect, Philip (later Sir Philip) Stott became lord of the manor at Stanton, and he spent the next thirty years repairing and improving the village. There is little point in mentioning individual buildings: the whole village with its 16th- and 17th-century houses reflects Stott's care.

Stanway In the parish church is a First World War memorial by Eric Gill, cut into the splay of a chancel window; and in the churchyard a memorial to Mary, Lady Wemyss (Mary Elcho), 1938, lettered by Eric Gill. In the village itself a magnificent war memorial of 1920, with lettering on the base by Eric Gill, a stone column and plinth by Sir Philip Stott and a bronze figure of St George and the Dragon by Alexander Fisher.

Weston-sub-Edge The lychgate to the church was designed by F. L. Griggs as a war memorial, c. 1919.

Willersey War memorial in the churchyard by F. L. Griggs, 1920; Willersey House, just south of the village, is of 1911-12 by Andrew Prentice, and part of it is a rebuilding of Top Farm, a 17th-century farmhouse which originally stood in the village itself.

Detail of the 1914-18 war memorial in St Peter's church, Stanway, by Eric Gill, 1920.

The Court Barn project

As you stand at the top of the steps coming out of St James's churchyard in Chipping Campden, the spectacular remains of Campden House are on your left. Just below you, built into the wall that flanks Campden House, is a 17th-century building so modest that you hardly notice it, Court Barn.

Court Barn, Church Street, Chipping Campden
(Photograph by Frank Johnson)

While using this book you may have felt that you were constantly being asked to imagine things that are not there, especially the objects and images which Arts and Crafts people created. I hope that in a few years time it will be easier to imagine the objects and images for, if the Court Barn project succeeds, the building will house work by, among others, C. R. Ashbee, F. L. Griggs, George Hart, Alec Miller, Gordon Russell and Paul Woodroffe; and, most remarkably, the entire working archive of Robert Welch, silversmith and designer.

The Court Barn project is being undertaken by the Guild of Handicraft Trust, which was founded in Chipping Campden in 1990 to foster the area's tradition of modern creativity. At the time of writing, the Trust has been offered a Development Grant by the National Lottery Fund to develop its plans for repairing Court Barn and adapting it as a museum and learning centre devoted to craft and design in the north Cotswolds in the 20th century and beyond. The project will create spaces for exhibitions, archive storage, a study area and a meeting room within the historic structure of the building.

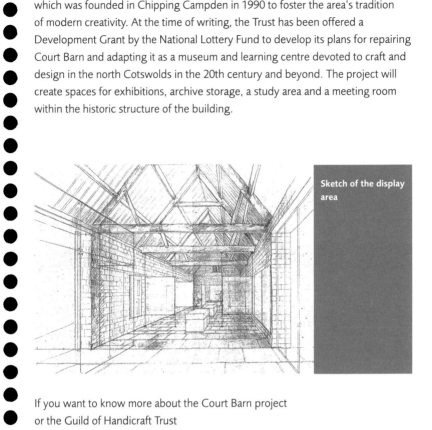

Sketch of the display area

If you want to know more about the Court Barn project
or the Guild of Handicraft Trust
please ring **+44 (0)1386 841417**
or e-mail **gofhtrust@ukonline.co.uk**

How to find out more

BOOKS

Gillian Naylor, *The Arts and Crafts movement: A study of its sources, ideals and influence on design theory* (London: Studio Vista, 1971)

Mary Greensted, *The Arts and Crafts movement in the Cotswolds* (Stroud: Alan Sutton, 1993)

Fiona MacCarthy, *The simple life: C. R. Ashbee in the Cotswolds* (London: Lund Humphries, 1981)

Alan Crawford, *C. R. Ashbee: Architect, designer and romantic socialist* (New Haven and London: Yale University Press, 1985)

Felicity Ashbee, *Janet Ashbee: Love, marriage and the Arts and Crafts movement* (Syracuse, N.Y.: Syracuse University Press, 2002)

Jerrold Northrop Moore, *F. L. Griggs (1876-1938): The architecture of dreams* (Oxford: Clarendon Press, 1999)

MUSEUMS

The most accessible public collection of the work of the Arts and Crafts movement is in Cheltenham Art Gallery and Museum. It is particularly strong in the work of Cotswold artist-craftsmen.

Index of people and places